WORLD
HISTORY SERIES ■ ■ ■

The History
of Slavery

Titles in the World History Series

The Age of Augustus
The Age of Feudalism
The Age of Pericles
The American Frontier
The American Revolution
Ancient Greece
The Ancient Near East
Architecture
Aztec Civilization
The Black Death
The Byzantine Empire
Caesar's Conquest of Gaul
The California Gold Rush
The Chinese Cultural
   Revolution
The Conquest of Mexico
The Crusades
The Cuban Missile Crisis
The Cuban Revolution
The Early Middle Ages
Egypt of the Pharaohs
Elizabethan England
The End of the Cold War
The French and Indian War
The French Revolution
The Glorious Revolution
The Great Depression
Greek and Roman Theater

The History of Slavery
Hitler's Reich
The Hundred Years' War
The Inquisition
The Italian Renaissance
The Late Middle Ages
The Lewis and Clark
   Expedition
The Mexican Revolution
The Mexican War of
   Independence
Modern Japan
The Punic Wars
The Reformation
The Relocation of the
   North American Indian
The Roman Empire
The Roman Republic
The Russian Revolution
The Scientific Revolution
The Spread of Islam
Traditional Africa
Traditional Japan
The Travels of Marco Polo
Twentieth Century Science
The Wars of the Roses
The Watts Riot
Women's Suffrage

WORLD
HISTORY SERIES ▪ ▪ ▪

The History
of Slavery

by
Norman L. Macht
and Mary Hull

Lucent Books, P.O. Box 289011, San Diego, CA 92198-9011

Y
326
m

Library of Congress Cataloging-in-Publication Data

Macht, Norman L. (Norman Lee), 1929–
    The history of slavery / by Norman L. Macht and Mary
Hull.
        p.   cm. — (World history series)
    Includes bibliographical references and index.
    Summary: Examines the practice of slavery as it existed in
early Mediterranean civilizations, during the Middle Ages, in
Africa, among Indians in the Americas, and in the United
States.
    ISBN 1-56006-302-5 (alk. paper)
    1. Slavery—History—Juvenile literature. [1. Slavery—
History.] I. Hull, Mary. II. Title. III. Series.
HT861.M23   1997
306.3'62'09—dc21   96–45640
                                                                    CIP
                                                                    AC

Copyright 1997 by Lucent Books, Inc., P.O. Box 289011,
San Diego, California 92198-9011

Printed in the U.S.A.

Contents

Foreword

Each year on the first day of school, nearly every history teacher faces the task of explaining why his or her students should study history. One logical answer to this question is that exploring what happened in our past explains how the things we often take for granted—our customs, ideas, and institutions—came to be. As statesman and historian Winston Churchill put it, "Every nation or group of nations has its own tale to tell. Knowledge of the trials and struggles is necessary to all who would comprehend the problems, perils, challenges, and opportunities which confront us today." Thus, a study of history puts modern ideas and institutions in perspective. For example, though the founders of the United States were talented and creative thinkers, they clearly did not invent the concept of democracy. Instead, they adapted some democratic ideas that had originated in ancient Greece and with which the Romans, the British, and others had experimented. An exploration of these cultures, then, reveals their very real connection to us through institutions that continue to shape our daily lives.

Another reason often given for studying history is the idea that lessons exist in the past from which contemporary societies can benefit and learn. This idea, although controversial, has always been an intriguing one for historians. Those that agree that society can benefit from the past often quote philosopher George Santayana's famous statement, "Those who cannot remember the past are condemned to repeat it." Historians who ascribe to Santayana's philosophy believe that, for example, studying the events that led up to the major world wars or other significant historical events would allow society to chart a different and more favorable course in the future.

Just as difficult as convincing students to realize the importance of studying history is the search for useful and interesting supplementary materials that present historical events in a context that can be easily understood. The volumes in Lucent Books' World History Series attempt to present a broad, balanced, and penetrating view of the march of history. Ancient Egypt's important wars and rulers, for example, are presented against the rich and colorful backdrop of Egyptian religious, social, and cultural developments. The series engages the reader by enhancing historical events with these cultural contexts. For example, in *Ancient Greece*, the text covers the role of women in that society. Slavery is discussed in *The Roman Empire*, as well as how slaves earned their freedom. The numerous and varied aspects of everyday life in these and other societies are explored in each volume of the series. Additionally, the series covers the major political, cultural, and philosophical ideas as the torch of civilization is passed from ancient Mesopotamia and Egypt, through Greece, Rome, Medieval Europe, and other world cultures, to the modern day.

The material in the series is formatted in a thorough, precise, and organized manner. Each volume offers the reader a comprehensive and clearly written overview of an important historical event or period. The topic under discussion is placed in a broad historical context. For example, *The Italian Renaissance* begins with a discussion of the High Middle Ages and the loss of central control that allowed certain Italian cities to develop artistically. The book ends by looking forward to the Reformation and interpreting the societal changes that grew out of the Renaissance. Thus, students are not only involved in an historical era, but also enveloped by the events leading up to that era and the events following it.

One important and unique feature in the World History Series is the primary and secondary source quotations that richly supplement each volume. These quotes are useful in a number of ways. First, they allow students access to sources they would not normally be exposed to because of the difficulty and obscurity of the original source. The quotations range from interesting anecdotes to farsighted cultural perspectives and are drawn from historical witnesses both past and present. Second, the quotes demonstrate how and where historians themselves derive their information on the past as they strive to reach a consensus on historical events. Lastly, all of the quotes are footnoted, familiarizing students with the citation process and allowing them to verify quotes and/or look up the original source if the quote piques their interest.

Finally, the books in the World History Series provide a detailed launching point for further research. Each book contains a bibliography specifically geared toward student research. A second, annotated bibliography introduces students to all the sources the author consulted when compiling the book. A chronology of important dates gives students an overview, at a glance, of the topic covered. Where applicable, a glossary of terms is included.

In short, the series is designed not only to acquaint readers with the basics of history, but also to make them aware that their lives are a part of an ongoing human saga. Perhaps they will then come to the same realization as famed historian Arnold Toynbee. In his monumental work, *A Study of History*, he wrote about becoming aware of history flowing through him in a mighty current, and of his own life "welling like a wave in the flow of this vast tide."

Important Dates in the History of Slavery

B.C. 4000   3000   2000   1000   A.D. 100   200   300   400   500   600   700   800   900

B.C.

ca. 4000
Sumerians settle in Mesopotamia with a slave labor force to do the heavy work.

ca. 3000
In Egypt, peasants are pressed into forced labor to build the pyramids.

ca. 100
Rome becomes one of the major slave-trading capitals of the world. The Roman legal code on slavery becomes the model for slavery laws in other societies.

72
The gladiator Spartacus leads a failed rebellion of Roman slaves.

A.D.

650
Muslim traders begin trade expeditions to sub-Saharan Africa; slave-trade networks are organized.

ca. 1200
The East African slave-trade network develops.

1204
Several prominent Venetian families start sugar plantations in Crete, stimulating the need for slave labor.

ca. 1250–1517
The Mamluks rule Egypt and import massive numbers of foreign slaves to fill their armies.

1266
The Genoese found a colony at Kaffa on the shores of the Black Sea. Kaffa becomes the major slave-trading center of the Late Middle Ages.

1348
The bubonic plague, or Black Death, decimates one-third of the European population and increases

Europe's need for foreign slaves. Italy increases its importation of domestic slave labor.

1492
Europeans see the profit potential of New World plantations as well as the need for imported slave labor when attempts to enslave indigenous peoples fail.

1500–1535
The Portuguese bring an estimated 10,000 to 12,000 African slaves to the market city of Elmina on the Gold Coast, near modern-day Accra, for resale.

ca. 1540
Ten thousand Africans per year are shackled and marched to the coast, where they are bartered to ship captains bound for the West Indies, Mexico, and South America.

| 1000 | 1100 | 1200 | 1300 | 1400 | 1500 | 1600 | 1700 | 1800 | 1900 | 2000 |

1619

The first Africans are brought to the Chesapeake Bay area of colonial Virginia.

1675–1677

King Philip's War, an Indian rebellion against English society in New England, claims the lives of many colonists and Indians. Following the victory of the settlers, captured Wampanoags, Nipmucks, and Narragansetts are sold as slaves and shipped to plantations in the West Indies.

August 14, 1791

Slaves in the French colony of San Domingo rise up and demand their independence. Toussaint-Louverture emerges as their leader and goes on to champion the islanders' independence.

1793

The invention of the cotton gin by school teacher Eli Whitney increases the demand for slaves as cotton production is streamlined.

August 22, 1831

Nat Turner's Rebellion, an uprising of 100 slaves, terrorized Southampton County, Virginia, killing 58 whites, mostly children.

1857

The Dred Scott decision is handed down by the U.S. Supreme Court. The decision ruled that an escaped slave did not gain freedom by reaching a free, or non-slave, state.

April 12, 1861

Confederates fire on Fort Sumter in the opening shots of the Civil War, in which slavery was a central issue.

January 1, 1863

The Emancipation Proclamation, written by President Abraham Lincoln in September 1862 to free slaves in the Confederate states, goes into effect.

1871

The free birth law is passed in Brazil, making the perpetuation of slavery difficult and paving the way for the 1888 abolition of slavery in Brazil.

1980

Mauritania passes its most recent ban on slavery, although slavery continues to persist, as it does in other North African countries today.

A Global Phenomenon

The history of slavery has no racial or geographic boundaries. Every race—black, brown, yellow, white, red—has been both slave and slave owner. Few nations or religions are exempt from the trade in human lives. People have enslaved others of their own nations, their own ethnic groups, their own races, their own religions, their own families. Even slaves have owned slaves. Whites enslaved their own neighbors and enemies. In Africa blacks who had never seen a white man made slaves of their black tribal foes. In Europe during the Middle Ages, Christian merchants made their fortunes by buying and selling slaves. Muslims used male slaves in armies and female and eunuch (castrated male) slaves in harems. Impoverished Chinese parents sold their children into slavery. There were slaves in the Indian cultures of Mexico and throughout North and South America thousands of years before the Vikings or Christopher Columbus knew that such places existed. Anybody, rich or poor, could wake up one morning a free person and go to sleep that night a slave. The fortunes of war, or simply being in the wrong place at the wrong time, often determined one's fate. Today's captor could be tomorrow's captive.

The word *slave* has its origins in *Slav*, the ethnic name for a group of people in central and eastern Europe who were heavily raided for slaves from the fifth to the thirteenth centuries. The word for *slave* in almost every Indo-European language comes from *Slav*. A slave is a person who is the property of another person or the government, a tool of labor in the same sense as a plow or a hammer or a mule. The slave's owner usually has complete control over the life and death of the slave. Like other forms of property, the slave could be bought, sold, or rented out to other masters. The conditions under which slaves have lived and worked, and the laws governing their ownership and treatment, have varied widely at different times and in different places. But the one common factor has been their bondage, or lack of freedom and control over their own lives. They were people—as human as their owners, and in many cases of equal or superior intelligence. But they remained chattel, or property, in the eyes of the law and society.

Nobody knows exactly when slavery began. But it has been part of human society since the beginning of recorded history. Only in the last few centuries has it been considered contrary to social laws and customs to buy and sell fellow humans. Matter-of-fact references to slaves as laborers appear in Genesis in the Bible.

Slaves were often used for agricultural work, such as harvesting sugar on this nineteenth-century American plantation.

Clay tablets unearthed in the region where the earliest settlements are believed to have been established—between the Tigris and Euphrates Rivers in what is now Iraq—prove the existence of slaves in the cities and valleys. Although we cannot pinpoint the year or even the century when slavery began, we can identify the conditions under which it flourished. Around seven thousand years ago people began to come together in villages that grew into towns and independent cities called city-states. They learned to construct buildings and to write, to make metal tools and to grow food. They tamed animals and raised them for skins, wool, milk, and meat. For the first time people could produce all the food they needed while remaining in a permanent home, instead of constantly moving about, hunting and gathering. However, this new way of life required many hands to work the fields. It became

practical to take captives in warfare instead of killing all the enemy warriors. Prisoners could be put to work tending the herds, growing the crops, and doing the household chores. Slaves could be worked from sunup to sundown year-round until they dropped. Except for their room and board, slaves cost nothing and were easily replaced. If they complained, rebelled, or tried to run away, they could be killed.

Slavery has been practiced on most continents and in almost every country, including the United States, where slavery was a legal institution until 1865. Slavery is a practice that can leave a painful legacy of injustice and inequality that many people would like to pretend never happened or no longer exists. However, slavery continues to be practiced in some parts of the world today, despite the fact that international law has forbidden its practice.

1 Slavery in Early Mediterranean Civilizations

Historians have speculated that the earliest civilizations in Mesopotamia, Egypt, Greece, and Rome could not have been built without the extensive use of slave labor. Nineteenth-century philosopher and economist Karl Marx went so far as to declare that all of Western civilization was built on the backs of slaves: "Without slavery, no Greek state, no Greek art or science; without slavery, no Roman Empire. Without Hellenism [Greek civilization] and the Roman Empire as the base, also no modern Europe."[1]

Mesopotamia, the earliest known civilization, was settled around 4000 B.C. by Sumerians who came from the east. As the first people to establish permanent agricultural communities with slaves to do the heavy work, they turned their attention to building cities. The Sumerians obtained slaves by kidnapping them from neighboring lands or capturing prisoners of war and forcing them into servitude. Debtors provided another source of slaves. If a man owed money or crops and could not pay, he might cancel the debt by selling himself or—because his wife and children were considered his property—his family into slavery for a limited number of years. If a man died owing money, his creditors could take his children as payment. And a slave born to slaves remained a slave for life. Educated and skilled artisans enslaved by the Sumerians worked as cooks, brewers, bakers, and potters, but slaves were most commonly used on construction projects. According to written records, slaves were used to build the Sumerian city of Ur. Explains Hans Baumann in *In the Land of Ur:*

> It was in building that the Sumerians reached some of their highest achievements. Instead of stone they used mud bricks, with asphalt as mortar. As there were great buildings erected in all the towns, the demand for bricks was enormous. . . . The biggest feats of construction were carried out by slave labor.[2]

In Africa, below the southern rim of the Mediterranean, the Egyptians built a society around the Nile River and its fertile banks. About 3000 B.C. the region became united under one ruler, called the pharaoh, whom the Egyptians considered divine. The pharaoh owned all the land and workshops and mines and quarries, and, in effect, all the people. Those who worked on the farms or in the shops did so at his pleasure. Unlike other societies, almost all the slaves in Egypt belonged to the ruler. Most of the slaves had been captured in wars or raids on nearby cities and tribes.

The abundance of peasants to work the farms, and the power of the pharaoh to press them into construction service whenever he wanted, made a slave class useful but not essential. If a pharaoh needed laborers in addition to his slaves to build a temple or a city or a pyramid, he would simply round up the farmers after the harvest and put them to work cutting and hauling the huge boulders of granite and marble. Then he would send them back to the fields when it was time for planting. This cycle of forced labor was known as corvée, or unpaid, labor. The monuments and pyramids that still stand in the desert were built in this way. According to Herodotus, the ancient Greek historian who visited Egypt and wrote of it in his *Histories:*

Cheops [the pharaoh] . . . compelled [his subjects] without exception to labor as slaves for his own advantage. Some were forced to drag blocks of stone from the quarries in the Arabian hills to the Nile, where they were ferried across and taken over by others, who hauled them to the Libyan hills. The work went on in three-monthly shifts, a hundred thousand men in a shift. It took ten years of this oppressive slave-labor to build the track along which the blocks were hauled—a work, in my opinion, of hardly less magnitude than the pyramid itself, for it is five furlongs [eleven hundred yards] in length, sixty feet wide, forty-eight feet high at its highest point, and constructed of polished stone blocks

This Egyptian engraving depicts slaves running while linked by a rope tied around their necks. Ancient Egyptian pharaohs controlled large slave classes, which worked the farms and constructed huge monuments and pyramids.

decorated with carvings of animals. To build it took, as I said, ten years—including the underground sepulchral [burial] chambers on the hill where the pyramids stand. . . . To build the pyramid itself took twenty years; it is square at the base, its height [eight hundred feet] equal to the length of each side; it is of polished stone blocks beautifully fitted, none of the blocks being less than thirty feet long.[3]

Such feats of construction could not have been accomplished if the pharaohs had not been able to harness the labor of their subjects and put so many thousands to work. The walls and roads of ancient Palestine were built using the slave labor of war captives. Naturally, kings, army officers, rich merchants, and farmers owned the most slaves.

In addition to public works projects, slaves also worked in the fields and took care of household chores. Many of these household slaves were treated as part of the family they belonged to, and sometimes they were adopted, made heirs, or freed by their masters. And under Hebrew law, a master who injured a slave had to set him free.

Greece

Slavery was an integral part of Greek society from its beginning. Of all the ancient civilizations, the Greek city-states were the first true slave society, dependent on slave labor to function and prosper. During the golden age of Athens in the fifth century B.C., when that city-state produced many great statesmen, poets, sculptors, histori-ans, and teachers, about half of the population of 155,000 were slaves.

Greece is a mountainous country, with few fertile flatlands or valleys. Because of this, ancient Greece prospered from the sea around it and from warfare, rather than agriculture. The community consisted of a small number of wealthy, powerful nobles; the rest were peasants, laborers, and slaves. As Greece evolved into individual, powerful, and rival city-states that were ruled by men who had become wealthy in industry and trade, slaves became a more important part of the economy. Slaves performed virtually all forms of labor, leaving the ruling class free to pursue the arts and sciences and to govern. Citizens of Athens considered business and trades, or working with their hands, beneath them, so slaves did most of those tasks, though not all Athenian households had slaves. A country farmer who sold his crops in the city might have a servant who worked with him in the fields, and if he were well-to-do, he would probably have a female servant to help his wife with the children and house. A woman rarely went out in public unless chaperoned by an elderly slave or servant. Slaves known as pedagogues, or teachers, would accompany children to school and wait for them until the lessons had ended. These slaves would also teach young Greek children how to dress, eat, and behave. Town craftsmen, such as shoemakers and armorers, usually had several slaves to help with the work.

Athenian slave society was relatively lenient. Athenian slaves talked often with freemen as equals and sometimes talked back to their masters. An Athenian writer known only as Old Oligarch wrote that

Building the Pyramids

According to the Greek historian Herodotus, *who traveled to Egypt and wrote about the pyramids in his* Histories, *the pharaoh Cheops pressed his subjects into service in order to build his pyramid, which was constructed one tier at a time. The cost of feeding and clothing the workers while they labored on Cheops's pyramid was astronomical.*

"The method employed [to build the pyramids] was to build it in tiers, or steps, if you prefer the word—something like battlements running up the slope of a hill; when the base was complete, the blocks for the first tier above it were lifted from ground level by cranes or sheerlegs, made of short timbers; on this first tier there was another lifting-crane which raised the blocks a stage higher, then yet another which raised them higher still. Each tier, or storey, had its crane—or it may be that they used the same one, which, being easy to carry, they shifted up from stage to stage as soon as its load was dropped into place. Both methods are mentioned, so I give them both here. The finishing-off of the pyramid was begun at the top and continued downwards, ending with the lowest parts nearest the ground. An inscription is cut upon it in Egyptian characters recording the amount spent on radishes, onions, and leeks for the laborers, and I remember distinctly that the interpreter who read me the inscriptions said the sum was 1600 talents of silver. If this is true, how much must have been spent in addition on bread and clothing for the laborers during all those years the building was going on—not to mention the time it took (not a little, I should think) to quarry and haul the stone, and to construct the underground chamber?"

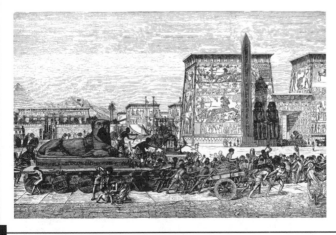

Even the basic necessities required to sustain the pharaoh's slaves, shown here hauling a huge carved figure, cost an enormous amount.

"slaves and metics [foreigners] in Athens lead a singularly undisciplined life; one may not strike them there, nor will a slave step aside for you."[4] Slaves in cities like Athens could not be distinguished from freemen or citizens. They wore the same clothes and worked alongside freemen in the trades. A master sometimes set up a clever slave in business for a share of the profits. Though technically the money a slave earned belonged to the master, the slave was usually allowed to keep part of his earnings. This money could eventually be used to purchase freedom. One Athenian slave who earned his freedom even went on to become the leading town banker. Because of his services to the state, the public assembly voted him citizenship.

Constant warfare in ancient Greece yielded thousands of prisoners of war who were used as slaves. Some of the least fortunate slaves might be forced to work in the silver mines of Athens. There they would crawl and lie in narrow tunnels only two or three feet high that were lighted by tiny oil lamps. The slaves worked ten-hour shifts, hacking the rocks with short-handled picks.

Persian, Indian, and African prisoners of war who were taken by Persian king Xerxes during his military campaigns ended up in Athenian households. Greek armies sometimes enslaved other Greeks, including the surviving women and children of their foes, during battles with rival city-states. These people might be exchanged for prisoners or ransomed to their families. Slave traders could purchase slaves in Asia Minor, Mesopotamia, Thrace, and southern Russia, then ship them to Greek markets. These prisoners, since they were not Greek-born, were considered a naturally lower form of life and therefore fit to be slaves. This order of things was described by the Greek philosopher Aristotle:

> Therefore all men who differ from one another by as much as the soul differs from the body or man from a wild beast (and that is the state of those who worked by using their bodies, and for whom that is the best they can do)—these people are slaves by

Greek citizens look over prisoners of war being sold as slaves. Ancient Greece depended on slaves to function; they did the manual labor while free citizens involved themselves in the arts, sciences, and government.

A slave holds up a mirror for a wealthy Greek woman. Female slaves in ancient Greece usually assisted the women of the house by doing chores and taking care of children.

nature, and it is better for them to be subject to this kind of control. . . . For a man who is able to belong to another person is by nature a slave.[5]

Rome

While the glory of Greece was at its pinnacle, the peninsula now known as Italy was inhabited by a mixture of tribes that had wandered and settled there from all directions. Most of them were farmers. Then, around 575 B.C., one of the more powerful tribes, the Etruscans, captured the small city of Rome and made it the capital of their kingdom. The people who lived in

and around the city gradually built up their own military strength, and after a hundred years of Etruscan rule, they threw out the occupiers. But they did not stop there. They went on to conquer most of the known world and establish Rome as the center of world trade. By 100 B.C. the Roman Empire comprised almost all the land around the Mediterranean Sea and everything from Britain in the west to Palestine in the east.

The Romans conquered people as well as land, and they used both as they saw fit. Like slaves in many other ancient societies, the Romans' captives were put to work building roads, bridges, walls, aqueducts (water channels), and public buildings. Commanders in the field had the power to decide which captives would be given to the soldiers as personal slaves, which would be ransomed, and which would be sold at public auction. Thousands of Briton, French, German, Moorish, Greek, Sicilian, and Palestinian men, women, and children were enslaved. Rome became the center of the slave trade for several hundred years. With little reliable evidence to go on, historians can only guess at the total slave population of Rome at any time. Their estimates range from as high as three slaves for every freeman to as low as one slave for every three freemen.

By 100 B.C. Rome had conquered Greece and replaced that dying cradle of democracy as the slave-trading capital of the world. The Romans devised a system of civil and criminal laws to govern the slave trade, the ownership and treatment of slaves, the rights and responsibilities of slave masters, and the means by which slaves might gain their freedom. These laws set a precedent for slave societies in the Muslim Middle East and eventually for the transatlantic slave trade fifteen hundred years later.

The Roman Empire organized and developed slavery as a regulated social institution. Large slave gangs provided the labor for farms and mines, and household servants did domestic labor. Some slaves were captives, but others were Roman citizens. A citizen could be enslaved for nonpayment of taxes, for example. In addition, poor parents could sell their children into slavery.

Many of the people the Romans conquered were from advanced Mediterranean societies, and they were highly educated. Slaves were often teachers and practitioners of medicine. The most elite corps of slaves served the emperor in the imperial palace, helping with the administration of the empire. In fact, the Roman Empire defined the term "civil servant," and slaves performed a variety of activities. Slaves staffed the bureaucracy needed to run the empire. They kept books, collected taxes, paid bills, ran libraries and

A Greek View of Slavery

The ancient Greek philosopher Aristotle wrote in his work Politics *that he believed some people were made to be slaves. Without a slave class, the ruling class of Greece could never have attained the cultured lifestyle that made it possible for Aristotle to write:*

"For all tame animals there is an advantage in being under human control, as this secures their survival. And as regards the relationship between male and female, the former is naturally superior, the latter inferior, the former rules and the latter is subject.

By analogy, the same must necessarily apply to mankind as a whole. Therefore all men who differ from one another by as much as the soul differs from the body or man from a wild beast (and that is the state of those who work by using their bodies, and for whom that is the best they can do)—these people are slaves by nature, and it is better for them to be subject to this kind of control, as it is better for the other creatures I have mentioned. For a man who is able to belong to another person is by nature a slave (for that is why he belongs to someone else). . . . Assistance regarding the necessities of life is provided by . . . slaves and by domestic animals. Nature must therefore have intended to make the bodies of free men and of slaves different also; slaves' bodies strong for the services they have to do, those of free men upright and not much use for that kind of work, but instead useful for community life."

This slave market shows the variety of slaves in the Roman Empire, including foreigners captured in war, poor Roman citizens, and children whose parents sold them into slavery.

the postal system, and oversaw the operation of the aqueducts, which had been built by slaves as well. Some worked alongside free workers in the trades to make bricks, glassware, pottery, metalwork, baked goods, and beer. Other slaves became foremen, managers, salesmen, and accountants and even traveled on behalf of their masters. Occasionally a slave would inherit his master's business. Many city slaves had the skills to become wealthy in business or industry—even to own their own slaves.

No matter how well slaves were treated, however, their masters still had to take measures to prevent them from escaping. As a result, many slaves were branded with telltale marks on their faces. Metal collars, like dog collars, were employed to identify slaves. The master's name was inscribed on the collar, and a reward would be offered for a slave's capture and return. Slaves who bore no brands or collars could still be identified by the foreign languages they spoke or by their accents. Though most slaves were

white like other Romans, their speech often differentiated them.

Most of the slaves who obtained their freedom bought it. Slaves could accumulate savings from gifts, by working outside the home or shop, and by earning a portion of the fee their masters received from renting slave services to others. Those slaves who were managers and business agents had expense accounts and handled money regularly. Another common means of gaining freedom was manumission, the practice of a master voluntarily releasing a slave from bondage. This could be gained in several ways. A master's last will and testament could free his slaves upon his death, although the state limited the number of slaves who could be freed in this way. A master could also free a female slave who had given birth to several children who remained slaves or as a reward for long and profitable service. Some owners cruelly freed old and sick slaves, thus relieving themselves of the burden of feeding and caring for them. These former slaves lived a

Roman slaves in cities often worked in businesses such as this as manufacturers, managers, salespeople, or accountants. Skilled slaves sometimes became wealthy enough to buy their own slaves.

meager existence on the daily portion of grain the state doled out to them and others in need. The state might grant a slave freedom for informing on criminals or reporting a crime against the state. The state would also set a slave free if he or she was physically mistreated. However slaves obtained their freedom, they had to meet certain obligations. Slaves who bought their freedom paid the going price for younger, stronger slaves to replace them. The master might require years of payments or free labor in addition to the cash price.

Freedom did not automatically make a former slave a full citizen of Rome. Mili-

tary or other civil service might eventually earn a former slave citizen status, but no former slave could hold public office or become an officer in the army.

The methods of obtaining freedom were different in rural areas, where gangs of slaves lived and worked together and tended to be treated with less respect. Mass rebellion, in which thousands of slaves overwhelmed their guards, was the only possible hope of freedom.

The Rebellion of Spartacus

Various revolts occurred over a seventy-year period in the early years of Roman rule, when large numbers of slaves were first brought to southern Italy and Sicily, and security and discipline were not yet established. The most famous of these rebellions was sparked by the Roman slave and rebel known as Spartacus. In 72 B.C. Spartacus led his fellow gladiators [professional fighters who engaged in a fight to the death for the public entertainment of Romans] in disarming their guards and attacking a nearby Roman military post. Spartacus hoped to persuade some pirate ships to sail them to freedom, but Roman troops caught up with them and wiped out the rebels. Their fate is described in *Slavery and the Slave Trade*:

> When the rebellion of Spartacus was finally crushed, 6000 crucified slaves lined the road from Capua to Rome; a grotesque reminder to all who saw it and to those who merely heard about it, of the futility of revolt and of the inevitable fate which awaited insurgent slaves.[6]

Worn-Out Cattle

Nowhere were slaves treated more harshly in the ancient world than in the Roman Empire, as evidenced by the words of the Roman statesman, soldier, and writer Cato (234–149 B.C.) as reported by Dorothy Mills in The Book of the Ancient Romans.

"The Roman was a hard and stern man; he did not spare himself, so why should he spare his slaves? They were to be cared for as long as they were useful to him, but then they were to be thrown to one side. Cato believed that 'worn-out cattle, sick sheep, broken tools, old and sick slaves and all other useless things should be sold.' He also gave instructions as to the food and clothing that should be given to the farm slave. In addition to his regular allowance, he might have a few of the 'olives that drop of themselves,' and a small quantity of sour wine. 'As for clothes, give out a tunic and a cloak once in two years. When you give a tunic or cloak, take back the old ones to make quilts. Once in two years good shoes should be given.'"

According to the Roman statesman, soldier, and writer Cato, slaves were like any other commodity— to be used as long as serviceable and then disposed of.

Slave revolts did not raise any public outcry to abolish slavery. It was accepted by all—philosophers, educators, and, later, the church—as part of the natural order of the universe. Uprisings were seen as violent outbreaks by prisoners and nothing more. Although the Catholic Church advocated more humane

A row of dangling, crucified corpses stretches along the Appian Way to the horizon as other participants in Spartacus's slave rebellion are added to the gruesome line.

treatment of slaves, it never sought manumission. In *The Many Faces of Slavery*, Israel E. Levine writes:

> Indeed, Christ himself accepted the institution of slavery. He believed that a slave was duty-bound to serve his master well. . . . While calling for humane treatment of slaves, the Church nevertheless felt that an individual's spiritual rather than bodily condition was important. Thus, bondage was tolerable as long as a slave could look forward to salvation after death. The Church, while it welcomed slaves into its ranks, did nothing to free them.[7]

The End of the Roman Empire

The problems involved in importing people of many different languages, customs, and cultures as slaves into a society that is foreign to them were recognized by Tacitus, a scribe of the time. Tacitus wrote, "Now that our households comprise tribes with customs the opposite of our own, with strange cults or none, you will never coerce [dominate] such a mixture of humanity, except by terror."[8] The importing of foreign slaves changed the nature of Roman society.

Although the Roman Empire lasted for a thousand years, it began to shrink long before its collapse. Its legions were unable to hold off invaders in the west. Gradually they lost what is now Germany, France, and England. In the east the Muslims chipped away at North Africa, Palestine, and Syria. But the heart of the empire remained intact. One of the reasons for the eventual decline of the empire was its lack of technological advancement, which was linked to its slave society. Generally the owners of the industries, from the state-owned cloth mills and mines to the small private pottery makers, reaped the profits but knew little about the industries they owned. The slaves, who did the work but got none of the profits, had no incentive to increase productivity through the use of innovative tools or methods. The same was true in the rural western part of the empire, where the slave gangs had no stake in increasing agricultural production.

As the empire declined, so did slavery, for military, health-related, and economic reasons. The end of the Roman wars of conquest eliminated a fertile source of slaves. A series of epidemics wiped out many slaves as well as free citizens. With little developed industry or commerce in the west, poor peasants in the outlying cities left their homes and tried to eke out survival on farms. Meanwhile, the loss of the city markets for their produce forced the landowners to disband their gangs of slaves, who were no longer profitable to feed and house. Serfdom developed, whereby masters divided their land into small plots and turned the slaves into tenant farmers who worked the land in

A shadowy, dungeonlike room houses slaves awaiting sale.

exchange for a portion of the crop. In this way the landowners were able to get free labor without the risks and costs associated with slaveholding. The new class of serfs that emerged from this system was no more free to leave their plots of land than the slaves had been. The serfs were economically bound to the landowners and legally bound to stay put by the state, which collected the taxes and recorded their existence in the census books.

The empire, which had covered millions of square miles from the rural west to the commercial and cultural centers of the east, had become a jumble of imperial decrees and local legal judgments. Laws passed by the Roman Senate were difficult to enforce throughout the territories. It had remained that way for about seven hundred years, until the sixth century A.D. Then the emperor Justinian created an organized body of laws, called the *Corpus Ju-ris Civilis* (Code of Civil Law), also known as the Justinian Code. The code unified the entire legal system and included a complete and detailed manual for the administration of a slave society. In the east, where the Roman Empire became known as the Byzantine Empire, the institution of slavery continued as it had at the peak of the Roman Empire's glory, under the Justinian Code. "Justinian's law code . . . had a crucial impact on the continuity of slavery in the western world," writes historian William D. Phillips Jr. "[The Romans] bequeathed to the medieval west an ongoing, if diminished, slave system and a sophisticated legal code with elaborate rules for operating such a system."[9]

The adoption of the Roman legal system for slavery by the Islamic nations of the Middle East and Africa provided the tracks upon which the engine of the slave trade would run for another thousand years.

2 Slavery During the Middle Ages

During the Middle Ages, the slave trade remained consistently lucrative throughout Europe, the Middle East, and Africa. Slaves were the principal export of the area that is now Eastern Europe and the main source of income. The slave markets were filled with Slavs, Turks, Russians, Indians, Circassians, North African Berbers, Moors, and sub-Saharan Africans. By land and sea, the slave trade routes moved west to east—to the world of Islam, which later replaced the Roman Empire as the largest slave society.

The Italian city-states of Genoa, Venice, Pisa, and Tuscany also became actively involved in the late-medieval slave trade. The Italian peninsula's central location put it in the middle of the trade routes between the rest of Europe and the Islamic world to the east and south. Italy's city-states flourished as a result of this trade, and the prosperity created by the slave trade generated a constant demand for slaves in Italian households.

Iris Origio, writing about a fourteenth-century Italian merchant, says, "By the end of the fourteenth century there was hardly a well-to-do household in Tuscany without at least one slave: brides brought them as part of their dowries, doctors accepted them in lieu [place] of fees—and it was not unusual to find them even in the service of a priest."[10] Since slaves were used primarily as domestic servants and concubines, almost all the slaves imported into Italy were women, and almost all were white, coming from as far away as Russia.

In the middle of the fourteenth century an epidemic of bubonic plague, known as the Black Death, swept through Europe and killed 25 to 30 percent of the population within three years. Death did not discriminate; it took the rich, the poor, and the slaves. As Europe rebuilt, those who survived found themselves with a bigger share of the wealth that remained, a surplus of work, and a shortage of labor. That combination created a greater demand for slaves and fueled the search for new sources of slave labor.

Slavery in Muslim Societies

Slavery was a part of the Arab world from its beginnings. The Arabs were the most active traders in black slaves from sub-Saharan Africa. They controlled the caravan routes that crisscrossed the Sahara from west to east and north to south. Because of the slave-trading activity, Islam spread to some of the desert dwellers and rulers of the African kingdoms south of

Medieval European households such as this used mainly female slaves imported from eastern Europe as domestic workers and concubines.

the desert, providing a religious and cultural bond. In eastern Africa Arab trading created a coastal language, known as Swahili, which is a mixture of Arabic and Bantu, a group of African languages. These religious and cultural bonds facilitated the slave trade, which required African rulers to supply slaves to the Arabs. It was an efficient network, comparable to the interstate highways of today, carrying goods from Europe and the Middle East into the heart of Africa, and African goods to the markets of Europe and the Middle East.

For more than three hundred years Arab traders brought to the African kingdoms dates, figs, sugar, cowries (shells used for currency), iron and copper tools and weapons, books, dyed fabrics, mirrors and glass, highly prized horses, and much-needed salt from the slave-worked salt mines of the Sahara. The Arabs took north with them ivory, animal skins, leather, pepper, ebony, cloves, kola nuts, and their most important products—gold and slaves. Approximately 18 million Africans were delivered into the Islamic trans-Saharan and Indian Ocean slave trades between the year 650 and the start of the twentieth century.

The hazardous slave-gathering journeys took two or three months in each direction. Without guides who could navigate by the sun and stars and find oases and pastures among the trackless shifting sand dunes, most caravans could not have survived the trek. Economic historian Anthony G. Hopkins describes the expeditions as

a feat of daring more impressive because it was repeated annually over many centuries. African and other merchants succeeded in creating an overland trade which, in size and organization, deserves to be ranked with the most famous achievements of merchant venturers in the era before industrialization removed the hardship from international commerce.[11]

For the slaves, the journey across the desert—at times searingly hot or freezing cold—the lack of water, and the burdens of carrying goods and unloading and loading the camels along the way, was as exhausting and dangerous as the later sea voyages.

Muslim societies in northern Africa and the Middle East used some slaves for agriculture, including sugar cultivation in Egypt and Morocco, but most of their slaves were used as domestic servants in homes or businesses and in the military. Some slave women became concubines or entertainers, living in harems containing hundreds of women, cut off from the outside world.

Treatment of slaves in Muslim societies ranged from decent to horrible. Under Islamic law it was illegal to separate mothers and daughters when slaves were sold. Slaves were more likely to be allowed to buy their freedom because the Koran, the Islamic holy book, advocated manumission, or freeing slaves: "Those your right hands own who seek emancipation, contract with them accordingly, if you know

Muslim traders march captive Africans to a slave market. The Muslims controlled African trade routes during the Middle Ages, bringing such goods as horses, salt, and fabric to African kingdoms in exchange for gold and slaves.

some good in them; and give them of the wealth of God that he has given you."[12]

In spite of this directive, however, slaves in Muslim societies were still looked on as inferior human beings. Laws that were intended to protect them were frequently ignored. A free Muslim could kill a slave, and the only penalty was payment of the slave's market price to his master. Masters could still mistreat, punish, or kill their slaves with impunity. A complex set of laws determined the fate of the children born to slaves. The status of the father determined if the child would be free or slave. Unlike the Romans, the Muslims used slaves in armies and to man the oars in navy galleys, or ships.

Muslim Slave Militaries and Christian Merchants

The Mamluks were slaves of Turkish descent who were brought to Egypt to serve in the armies of the caliph, or ruler. Because of the widespread use of slave labor in the Egyptian military, the term *Mamluk*, which means "owned" or "men who have been bought" in Arabic, came to signify a white or Asian slave living in an Islamic state. After being trained as soldiers, the Mamluks ruled over local populations in the name of the caliph and eventually grew powerful enough to challenge their masters. The Mamluks themselves ruled Egypt from 1250 to 1517, and they contin-

Women tied together with rope are led to a boat to be sold as slaves to Muslims. Female slaves were used as domestic workers, entertainers, or concubines.

Eunuchs Were Prized as Slaves

Jahiz, a ninth-century Muslim, explained why eunuchs were so highly prized as servants in his Book of Animals, *quoted in* Slavery from Roman Times to the Early Transatlantic Trade *by William Phillips.*

"Another change which overcomes the eunuch; of two slaves of Slavic race, who are . . . twins, one castrated and the other not, the eunuch becomes more disposed toward service, wiser, more able, and apt for the various problems of manual labor, and you find him more lively in intelligence and conversation. All these qualities result only in the castrated one. On the other hand, his brother continues to have the same native torpor [sluggishness], the same lack of natural talent, the same imbecility common to slaves, and incapacity for learning a foreign language."

ued to employ slave labor in their armies. The Mamluks relied on foreign slaves and the slave markets around the Black Sea to fill their armies. However, by 1260 the caravan routes between Mamluk territory and the Black Sea slave markets had been blocked by the Mongol ruler Hülegü Khan. Hülegü hoped to prevent the Mamluks from replenishing their armies, making it easier for him to conquer them.

By 1261, just as the Mamluk armies were reeling from lack of recruits, merchants from the Italian city-state of Genoa negotiated a treaty with the Byzantine emperor, Palaeologus, that gave them a virtual monopoly on the Black Sea trade. Genoese merchants, whose navy now controlled the Black Sea, began selling slaves to the Mamluks, using the sea route that connected Egypt to the Crimea by the Bosporus strait.

The Genoese, who had earlier helped the crusaders attack the Mamluks, now became their commercial ally. By 1266 the Genoese had a thriving colony formed at Kaffa on the shores of the Black Sea, and they had become the most important supplier of slaves for the Muslim armies of the Mamluks.

The slave market at Kaffa, where the majority of slaves traded were Slavs or Circassians, became the major slave-trading center of the Late Middle Ages. When Spanish writer Pero Tafur visited Kaffa in the mid–fifteenth century, the number of slaves shipped from there annually was estimated at two thousand. Tafur described the slave auctions:

In this city [Kaffa] they sell more slaves both men and female, than anywhere else in the world. . . . I bought there two female slaves and a male, whom I still have in Cordova [Spain] with their children. The selling takes place as follows. The sellers make the slaves strip to the skin, male as well as females, and they put on them a cloak of felt,

Slavery in the World of Islam

Historian William Phillips writes about slave marriages in Muslim societies in his book Slavery from Roman Times to the Early Transatlantic Trade.

"Marriages between free Muslims and slave women were common, and the offspring of such unions enjoyed full freedom. In the Koran, in fact, marriage with a pious slave woman was regarded as much more suitable than with an unbeliever. The most spectacular cases of free-slave marriages involved the Abbasid caliphs [eighth to eleventh centuries]. Hoping to avoid any family alliances and the particularism this might engender [produce], the Abbasids adopted many aspects of the Near Eastern concept of the exalted god-king. As part of their attempt to create the largest possible distance between themselves and their subjects, they proclaimed that no one was equal to them. Because no marriage could possibly add luster to their station, the Abbasid caliphs married slave wives, with the result that after [A.D.] 800 not a single caliph was born the son of a free mother.

Muslim males kept their female dependents isolated from the world, segregated in a special portion of the house known as the harem. There the women could entertain their own guests, but they could only venture out for specific purposes. Most free Muslims could afford no more than a single wife; only the wealthiest could carry the harem system to extremes. One such example was provided by . . . al-Malik al-Afdal [1094–1121], who left eight hundred slave concubines in his harem when he died. To give an idea of his jealousy, he is reported to have beheaded one mistress on the spot for looking out of a window of the harem while in his presence."

and the price is named. Afterward, they throw off the coverings, and make them walk up and down to show whether they have any bodily defect.[13]

Kaffa's location on the Black Sea was strategic. The Black Sea basin area has been described by historians as a "population reservoir" for the slave trade. The majority of slaves sold at Kaffa were Slavs or central Asian peoples from Khazaria, Circassia, or the Caucasus. In the 1289–1290 notebooks of Lamberto di Sambuceto, the notary of Kaffa, there are numerous entries detailing the sale of slaves by Genoese merchants. These legal documents are among the only sources for the personal histories of the thousands of otherwise unchronicled people who were traded like furs and spices at Kaffa. The following excerpt from Sambuceto's notebook presents a picture of what the market may have been like:

21 May 1289: Jacobus Bocharius sells to Ansaldus Usumaris a boy slave with blond hair, named Michaal, aged 8 years, for a price of 290 aspres baricats [unit of money].

A Muslim merchant keeps an eye on his slaves for sale through a large window.

Traders discuss the sale of a female slave. Muslim men often married their female slaves; the richest men sometimes accumulated large harems of wives.

26 May 1289: Luchetus de Lorto sells to the furrier Enricus de Serrinoune, a female Circassian slave with olive complecion, named Crestinna, aged 13 years, for a price of 600 aspres baricats.

23 May 1290: Simon de Sygestro sells to Fredercius Panzanus a white Khazarian female slave, named Coxani, aged approximately 11 years, for a price of 470 aspres baricats.

23 June 1290: Jeracharona, wife of Machometus, sells to Obertus de Plebe and to Obertus de Gavio, a Russian female slave, called Margarita, aged 12 years, for a price of 400 aspres baricats.

1 August 1290: Ferrarius de Varagine sells to Baldus Marach of Vulturo, a male Khazarian slave, aged 5 years, for a price of 175 aspres baricats.[14]

In Sambuceto's notebooks from 1289 to 1290 there are over sixty recorded instances of slaves being sold to Genoese

Becoming a Slave in the Middle Ages

The thirteenth-century traveling merchant Marco Polo left a record of his experiences in Europe and Asia. Polo encountered numerous slaves and wrote about some of the ways people became slaves. The following excerpt is from The Travels of Marco Polo, *edited by Ronald Latham.*

"[The people of Bengal, India,] are great traders, exporting spikenard, ginger, sugar, and many other precious spices. The Indians come here and buy the eunuchs of whom I have spoken, who are very plentiful here because any prisoners that are taken are immediately castrated and afterwards sold as slaves. So merchants buy many eunuchs in this province and also many slave girls and then export them for sale in many other countries. . . .

In the province of Manzi [China] almost all the poor and needy sell some of their sons and daughters to the rich and noble, so that they may support themselves on the price paid for them and the children may be better fed in their new homes. . . .

While [the Russians] engage in stravitza [huge drinking bouts], they borrow money on the security of their children from merchants who come from Khazaria, Sudak, and other neighboring countries, and then spend it on drink, and so they sell their own children."

Marco Polo's business travel allowed him to observe slavery in several parts of the world.

Muslim traders examine their human merchandise before making the sale. The Mamluks purchased many slaves for their armies and harems from the Genoese market at Kaffa.

people, but there are only three instances of manumission. One of these manumissions appears not to have been a manumission at all: "Baldus de Vulture frees his slave Jacobus, bought from Ferrarius of Varagine, on the condition that he serve the Armenian Stephanus and his wife all during their lives."[15] Merchants in Kaffa were in the business of trading, not freeing, slaves.

Genoese merchants continued to be the dominant supplier of male slaves for the Mamluk military and female and eunuch slaves for Mamluk harems until 1400, when the overland caravan routes connecting Mesopotamia and Mamluk Syria reopened. While the majority of the slaves purchased by the Genoese and sold at Kaffa went to the Mamluk armies, many were also imported to the Italian city-states for resale as domestic slaves.

Domestic Slavery in the Italian City-States

Although the Catholic Church tried to restrict the sale of slaves in Italy to non-Christians, merchants who imported eastern European Christian slaves simply passed them off as Muslims or forced them to change their religion. As with the Genoese and Mamluk alliance, economic concerns took precedence over religious ones. Non-Christian slaves were baptized and given Christian names after being bought by Italian families for use as servants.

The majority of slaves imported into the Italian city-states were young women, many of whom became concubines for their masters. There were laws concerning the course of action to be taken in the case of a pregnant slave. A master who impregnated a slave could arrange a marriage for her, sell her, raise the child as a slave, or free the slave and marry her. In 1427 Cosimo de' Medici of Florence was known to have had a son by a Circassian slave girl. This boy was later legitimized and went on to become the archpriest of

Italian merchants dominated trade in the Black Sea. The prosperous Genoese slave market at Kaffa provided slaves for Italian families and Mamluk harems and armies.

Prato.[16] In addition to being used for domestic service or concubinage, slaves could be pledged for loans or rented to craftsmen in order to enhance their value.

In the Italian city-states, however, manumission was a more common occurrence, especially upon the death of a slave's master: "3 July 1290: Rollandus de Robino had made his will. He wishes to be buried in the church of St. Francis in Caffa; he grants several bequests: he frees his slave Margarita, counts up his debit accounts, and designates his heir, Donatus de Quarto."[17]

Other avenues to freedom, such as marriage to an Italian citizen, and more drastic measures, such as running away or even suicide, were also used by slaves. For those manumitted slaves who chose to remain in Italy, it was possible to become assimilated into the society, as evidenced by Venetian traveler Marco Polo's slave Peter, a Tartar, who was manumitted in 1324 and granted full rights of citizenship by the Venetian Republic. The Slavs, Hungarians, Russians, Tartars, Circassians, Khazarians, Africans, and other peoples who unwittingly found their way to countries other than their homelands were forced to adapt to their new situations. African slaves who began to be imported into the New World as early as the 1500s found themselves in similar circumstances.

Sugar and Slavery

More than anything else, the primary factor that led to the transatlantic trade in black slaves was the introduction of sugar to western Europe during the Middle

Ages. As the demand for sugar soared in Europe in the sixteenth and early seventeenth centuries, European investors developed vast new sugar cane plantations and refineries in the tropical climate of the Caribbean islands and Central and South America. They began to import African labor to work these plantations.

Sugar had been relatively unknown in most of western Europe prior to the Crusades, as the major sweeteners were honey and fruit juices. The crusaders encountered refined sugar in Syria and Palestine, and after defeating the Muslims, they took over the sugar production and refining facilities in the Holy Land. When the refined sugar reached the markets of western Europe, consumers could not get enough of it. When the Muslims later drove the crusaders out of the Holy Land in the thirteenth century, they continued to supply sugar to Europe. Sixty-six sugar mills prospered in Cairo alone.

Christian merchants, however, took sugar cane plants with them and began growing cane on Mediterranean islands and eventually in the Canary Islands and Madeira, in the Atlantic Ocean off the coast of Africa. When Crete became a Venetian colony after the defeat of the Muslims in the Fourth Crusade (1202–1204), some of Venice's most prominent families started sugar plantations there. The increased demand for sugar in Europe stimulated the use of slaves. The Italian colonies of Crete and Cyprus became the chief suppliers of sugar to Europe, a position they held until the more efficient sugar producers of the early transatlantic trade began to undersell them.

Mediterranean sugar production relied on slave labor, although not exclusively. Slave labor, in addition to a corvée on peasants, was practiced on Crete and Cyprus, most noticeably after the plague of 1348, which depleted available agricultural laborers and increased the islands' dependence on slaves imported from the shores of the Black Sea. Scholars argue that Mamluk sugar cultivation in Egypt and Morocco also used slave labor, since many of the place names in valleys where sugar was known to be cultivated incorporate the word *slave*. The search for labor for the sugar industry was one of the motives behind the Moroccan trans-Saharan slave expeditions of the 1500s. Similarly, the slave-sugar economy of the Mediterranean developed a model in the European mind for plantation slavery in the New World. When sugar cane was planted on Mediterranean islands, the seeds of a new slave society, this time black, were also sown.

3 Slavery in Africa

Africa is an enormous continent—three times as large as the United States—but the vast Sahara splits Africa into two different regions, northern Africa and sub-Saharan Africa. The lands to the north, bordering on the Mediterranean, were populated by indigenous groups of Berbers, Arabs, and Semites. These people were active traders with the ports around the inland sea, exchanging goods and cultural influences. The area below the Sahara ranged from arid plains to humid tropical forests near the equator to thousands of miles of open grasslands. Sub-Saharan Africa was home to hundreds of ethnic groups from different cultural and linguistic backgrounds. The region was divided among kingdoms, empires, and superstates, some more advanced and powerful than others. In a world where land could be hostile and unproductive, power rested more in having control over people than in owning real estate.

The Venetian explorer Cadamosto, who visited Senegal in the 1450s, wrote of the presence of slavery and slave trading in West Africa:

> The King lives thus: he has no fixed income [from taxes]: save that each year the lords of the country, in order to

A person of rank in the Congo is carried by his slaves. Sub-Saharan Africa was populated by many different ethnic groups, some of which dominated others and formed kingdoms.

African tribes took captives from one another to use as slaves, as depicted in this illustration. Some were retained by their captors to work in farming and mining, and the rest were sold to traders.

stand well with him, present him with horses, which are much esteemed owing to their scarcity, forage beasts such as cows and goats, vegetables, millet [a grain], and the like. The King supports himself by raids, which result in many slaves from his own as well as neighboring countries. He employs these slaves [in many ways, but mainly] in cultivating the land allotted to him: but he also sells many to the Azanaghi and Arab merchants in return for horses and other goods, and also to Christians, since they have begun to trade with these blacks.[18]

When Islamic traders and, later, Europeans arrived to tap the supply of slave labor that sub-Saharan Africa offered, they found a system and a way of life ready to accommodate them.

Slavery occurred in both northern and sub-Saharan Africa, ranging from societies that owned slaves to large-scale slave societies similar to those of Greece and Rome, where slaves were employed in specific industries and occupations. Africans used slave labor for agricultural production, clearing land, and mining. In his book *The Lake Regions of Central Africa*, published in 1860, British explorer Richard Burton described the tradition of slave trading among the Africans with whom he came in contact:

All African wars are for one of two objects: cattle lifting and kidnapping. . . . The process of kidnapping, an inveterate [established] custom in these lands, is in every way agreeable to the mind of a man-hunter. A poor and powerful chief will not allow his neighbors to rest wealthier than himself; a quarrel is soon found, the stronger attacks the weaker, hunts and harries [harasses] his cattle, burns his villages, carries off his subjects and sells them to the first passing caravan.[19]

Not all the enslaved captives were sold. Those retained were used for domestic service and in the over forty thousand gold mines of people like the Ashanti, a powerful West African tribe. Domestic slavery was in many ways a kinder, more humane institution within Africa than in the New World. Slaves, while not completely adopted as kinsmen, became members of a household. They had the right to marry, raise families, and own property, including their own slaves. The more skilled his work, the higher the slave's standing. Some slaves worked as blacksmiths, making weapons. Others built canoes and manned them, cared for a master's horses, or if employed by a king, they might serve as royal bodyguards. However, in the mines and on agricultural plantations, slave life was harsh. In the area that is now Nigeria, the Ibo and the Ashanti drove their slaves relentlessly, replacing those who died by raiding weaker tribes and by purchasing slaves from markets.

Some African ethnic groups used slaves for human sacrifices. The Ashanti kingdom along the Gold Coast of western Africa sacrificed slaves as part of a ritual associated with the deaths of important persons. Similar reasoning was used in the mass sacrifices of slaves upon the death of a pharaoh in ancient Egypt. The belief behind the sacrifices was that deceased members would suffer no inconveniences in their new homes, as they would have familiar people with them who could minister to their needs. According to Captain A. B. Ellis of Great Britain's West India Regiment, who wrote about the Ashanti,

> The number of persons sacrificed depends upon the wealth and rank of the deceased; but the favourite wives and most trusted slaves are, beyond

the Colonial boundary, almost invariably immolated at the demise of their lord. The greatest slaughter takes place at the decease of a king of Ashanti, and scores of human beings are sacrificed whenever a member of the royal family dies.[20]

Slave dealers like this one sold slaves to Muslims, Europeans, and other Africans. Tribes like the Ashanti on the west coast of Africa used slaves for mass sacrifice when an important member of the tribe died.

African and Arab Trade Networks

When the Berbers and other Muslim traders of the north crossed the Sahara and made trade links with the kingdoms to the south, they found willing trade partners. Sub-Saharan Africa had gold, ivory, salt, cloves, animal skins, ebony, copper, kola nuts, and slaves, for which the Arabs had ready markets. African chiefs, who preferred to keep female slaves and sell the males, traded for European guns, gunpowder, fabrics, brandy, and horses. One horse could be exchanged for as many as ten to fifteen slaves. According to historian William D. Phillips:

> The exchange of horses for slaves tended to become a circular process: horses were purchased with slaves, and then could be used in military operations which yielded further slaves, and financed further purchases of horses. Trade and war thus fed upon each other in a self-sustaining process.[21]

The Arab and Berber traders of North Africa who engaged in the Saharan trade encountered many obstacles to their commerce and had to brave incredible hardship. Trans-Saharan journeys required elaborate planning and foresight. In *Slavery from Roman Times to the Early Transatlantic Trade*, William Phillips explains the logistics of caravan desert crossings:

> Many merchants traveled with each caravan, with four camels per merchant, one for food and water and three to carry the merchandise. The caravan leader (usually called the khabir) was vested with the full authority to direct the caravan and to handle the varied business dealings that were its reason for existence. Although the leader hired guides as the caravan traversed each section of the route, he still had to be a navigator in his own right. Skilled guides and leaders could tell the correct path not only by the sun and the stars, but also by the smell and touch of the sand and the local vegetation. Each caravan carried its own scribe to keep the business records and messengers to carry orders up and down the line of march. On the route, aside from the necessary chores of pasturing and watering the camels at night and getting them ready to move in the morning, there were human obstacles to overcome. Each oasis charged a fee, and local chieftains would often charge transit duties or insist that local guides be hired (often thinly disguised bribery). There was an annual pattern to the movement of the caravans. They generally spent the winter in the Sudan, and this required them to leave North Africa in September or October and begin their return journey in April or May. By following this schedule they could hope to avoid the summer's heat and the equally hazardous winter cold of the desert. In the mid–fourteenth century, the Moroccan traveler Ibn Batutta encountered a heavy snowstorm on the last leg of his return journey from the Sudan to Morocco. Travelers might be caught at any time by sandstorms that destroyed the path, cruelly afflicted humans and animals, and scattered the caravan. If things went well, they could count on making the crossing in two or three months.[22]

Muslim slave traders lead a caravan of bound captives. The Arab and Berber merchants who crossed Africa trading goods for slaves planned the hazardous journeys carefully to avoid extreme weather conditions.

If they were fortunate, the caravans made a successful return journey with slaves, gold, and other sub-Saharan exports to resell in the north. Among the players in the West African slave trade were the Muslim group from the western Sudan known as the Wangara, who had established a series of trading stations along the forest country. The Wangara supplied labor for the Akan, a West African ethnic group, traveling into their hinterlands and purchasing gold with slaves and other goods. The Wangara obtained slaves by kidnapping rural African people or, in some instances, by purchasing them from areas where population pressures and overcrowding had forced families to sell their children. The Wangara had to continue to supply the Akan with slaves if they wished to obtain gold. The Akan were discreet about their gold mines and their mining techniques; they were careful to prevent foreigners from learning the location of gold mines for fear of invasion.

Muslim traders also penetrated Africa's eastern coast, creating trade networks based on the exchange of slaves.

Zanzibar and the East African Slave Trade

The East African slave-trading network developed to meet the demand for slaves to work the clove plantations on the islands of Zanzibar and Pemba, as well as other mainland agricultural enterprises, which were organized as early as the 1200s. Muslims from the Arabian Peninsula and Persia began to visit East Africa as early as the eighth century A.D. Sailing down the coast in their dhows, they came to trade glassware, ironware, textiles, wheat, and wine in exchange for slaves, ivory, skins, and other animal products. Many Arabs settled along the coast, giving rise to the Swahili people, a coastal group of mixed Arab and African descent. The Swahili were avid traders and outfitted slave caravans for expeditions to the African interior.

The Swahili traders bartered ammunition, weapons, and other goods for slaves and ivory, which they would bring back to the coast for resale. They also hired inland tribes to round up captives and march them to the eastern coast. Between the forced marches to the coast and the subsequent sea voyages, many of the slaves perished before reaching their final destination.

A British missionary described the effects of the debilitating trek of slaves from the interior to the coast:

It is like sending up for a large block of ice to London in the hot weather. You know that a certain amount will melt away before it reaches you in the country; but that which remains will be quite sufficient for your wants. I have no reason to doubt that four or five lives are lost for every slave sold in Zanzibar.[23]

East Africa's commercial development caused an enormous increase in the slave trade by 1800. According to economic

---

Human Sacrifice Among the Akan

Pieter de Marees, a Fleming who traded on Africa's Gold Coast in the sixteenth century, published an account of the ethnic groups with whom he came into contact. The following description by Marees from Pieter de Marees: A Description and Historical Account of the Gold Kingdom of Guinea, 1602, *written by A. van Dantzig and A. Jones, reveals the Akan theory of afterlife as well as the rationale for ritual human sacrifice to the deceased.*

"We asked where they go and where their body journeys when they have passed away and are dead. They answered that it is quite dead and they do not know of any resurrection on the Last day, as we do. They do know that they go to another world when they die (although they do not know where) and in that respect their condition is different from that of the Animals; but they are unable to explain to you the place where they go, whether it is under the ground or up in the Heaven. When they die, people make much show of giving them one thing and another [to take] along, which clearly indicates that they have a feeling that after this life there is another and that there too, one has all sorts of things to do, as on earth.

As a King needs more services than an ordinary person, many people also have to journey with him, accompany him on the way and serve him in the other World; for as he is undertaking a great journey, he will need all sorts of things. . . . Furthermore, any nobleman who may have served the King during his lifetime will present to him when he has died a Slave to serve him; other Men also offer one of their Wives to serve him and to cook his food; others bring their son in order that he may journey to the other World with the King; and all these persons are killed and decapitated."

historian Philip Curtin, this development represented an increase and change in the ancient interior-coastal slave trade that would ultimately lead to European colonialism in Africa:

> These new caravans from the coast were not so much a replacement of the established caravans from the interior as a supplement, competing along the same routes. It was simply the entry of new firms—and to some degree of new technology, since the coastal caravans were far better armed than caravans had been in the past. Along with the new entrants came a new level of violence. The coastal caravan leader sometimes raided for slaves, rather than buying those offered on the market. They also furnished arms to African political authorities with the intention that they, in turn, would use them to kill elephants and capture slaves. This new phase was the begin-

ning of a transition ultimately traceable to the start of industrialization in Europe, and one that was to end with the European conquest of most of Africa by the end of the century.[24]

When a trader arrived in Zanzibar with a new caravan of slaves, ivory, and other goods, much enthusiasm was generated on the island, and the market square would be crowded with spectators, local buyers, and dhow captains. Before their sale, the slaves would be washed and greased with coconut oil to make their bodies shine. In addition, young and beautiful girls would be made up and wrapped in colorful cloth. They might be given gold ear and nose rings, bracelets, or anklets, which would be removed after the sale was made. Wholesale traders sold slaves in lots, rather than individually, and placed them in cages that were twenty feet square. As many as 150 slaves could go into one cage. The cages generally con-

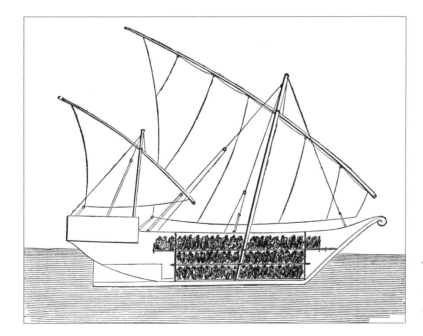

Slaves crowded into a dhow are barely distinguishable from one another. The dhows sailed along the east coast of Africa, transporting slaves purchased in Zanzibar to other markets for resale.

Africa

tained a mixture of ages, sexes, and physical conditions. Husbands and wives were often separated because buyers might find them troublesome together. Attractive young women received special attention, as they were capable of fetching high prices as concubines. Young healthy girls also had good reproductive value and fetched high prices, for their offspring would automatically become the property of their master. Young healthy boys fetched high prices as prime candidates for castration, which was performed at a center in Zanzibar after a boy was sold. Because the survival rate of the castration operation was low, only healthy-looking boys were chosen to undergo the procedure. Slave owners from many different cultures believed that male slaves who were castrated made more obedient servants, and centers for performing castration operations existed in Africa, the Middle East, and Europe.

Slavery had always been part of the African culture, but as Europeans became involved in the slave trade, the profit motive and the massive demands of outside markets began to turn Africa into a continent of greater carnage and decimation.

European Involvement

By the early 1400s the Portuguese, who were renowned for their navigational abilities, were sailing far to the west in search of tuna, whales, and sardines. Portugal's ruler earned the nickname Henry the Navigator for his efforts in exploration; he put his best boatbuilders, astronomers, and mapmakers to work studying the stars, ocean currents, winds, and tides to extend their explorations beyond the Mediterranean. He learned from the Arabs, who brought back from China the secrets of building sturdier ships to withstand rough ocean seas and the tricks of sailing against the wind. Until then sailors had feared that if they sailed away with the prevailing wind, they would be unable to return home sailing into those same winds.

Determined to extend his influence to the south, Prince Henry sent his sailors along the previously unexplored bulging Atlantic coast of northern Africa. In 1441 they landed on the seemingly deserted coast. When they came upon a group of black natives, they captured twelve of them and took them back to Portugal. Although Prince Henry was searching for gold, he also had a need for slaves to work Portugal's busy sugar plantations and refineries on the islands off Europe and West Africa. Enthused at the prospect of an unlimited supply of slaves to work the sugar cane fields, he sought the approval of the pope, who wielded great influence in such matters. For years the kings of

Slaves March to the Coast from the African Interior

A British missionary encountered the infamous Arab trader Tippu Tip's slave caravan on its annual march from the interior to the market at Zanzibar. The missionary sent indignant protests to both Zanzibar and England. Leda Farant's Tippu Tip and the East African Slave Trade *contains his account.*

"It is difficult adequately to describe the filthy state of their bodies; in many instances not only scarred by the cut of a 'chikote' [a piece of hide used to enforce obedience], but feet and shoulders were a mass of open sores, made more painful by the swarms of flies which followed the march and lived on the flowing blood. They presented a moving picture of utter misery, and one could not help wondering how any of them had survived the long tramp from the Upper Congo, at least 1000 miles distant. . . . The head-men in charge were most polite to us as they passed our camp. Each was armed with a rifle, a knife, and spear, and although decently clothed in clean cotton garments, they presented a thoroughly villainous appearance. Addressing one, I pointed out that many of the slaves were unfit to carry loads. To this he smilingly replied 'They have no choice! They must go, or die!' Then ensued the following conversation: 'What do you do if they become too ill to travel?' 'Spear them at once!' was the fiendish reply. . . . 'I see women carrying not only a child . . . but in addition, a tusk of ivory or other burden. . . . What do you do in their case when they become too weak to carry both? . . . Who carries the ivory?' 'She does! We cannot leave valuable ivory on the road. We spear the child and make her burden lighter. Ivory first, child afterwards!'"

Slave journeys from the interior of Africa to Zanzibar (pictured) were torturous: Slaves were beaten, plagued by insects, hampered by heavy loads, and killed when they became too weak to continue.

A chained and collared slave gang in Zanzibar carries baskets while a Muslim trader stands guard. The Zanzibar market sold slaves wholesale; slaves crammed into a cage were sold as a lot instead of individually.

Portugal had regarded the pope as a feudal overlord within their realms and sought his advice. The support of the pope was necessary, for the Catholic Church wielded the power of excommunication, which was banishment from the church and its rites. If the Portuguese ruler fell out of favor with the pope and became excommunicated, his own subjects could turn against him, and other countries might wage war on Portugal in the name of the church. The pope gave Prince Henry his blessing to take back Africans as slaves. As a result, more than nine hundred Africans had been seized and brought to Lisbon as slaves by 1448. As the slave trade reached about one

thousand people a year, the Portuguese built a fort on an island off what is now Mauritania to imprison the slaves awaiting transport. But the Portuguese were not the only Europeans trading with Africa. Soon a half dozen other European nations set up their own forts and trading posts off the coast of Africa. Their primary interest was gold, not slaves. The Portuguese continued to push farther south down the coast, reaching the Bantu kingdom in the Congo, where they formed an alliance that supplied them with a steady flow of slaves.

Portuguese traveler Duarte Pacheco Pereira, who wrote his travel account *Esmeraldo de Situ Orbis* between 1505 and

Slave Markets in Zanzibar

Captain Smee, an Englishman, was sent to the East African coast in 1811 by the British Indian government, on a "voyage of research." Captain Smee was the first Englishman to report on the Zanzibar slave markets. Leda Farant's Tippu Tip and the East African Slave Trade *contains his account of the methods of sale.*

"The slaves are ranged in a line commencing with the youngest and increasing to the rear according to their size and age. At the head of this file, which is composed of all sexes and ages from six to sixty, walks the person who owns them. Behind and at each side two or three of his domestic slaves, armed with swords and spears, serve as guards. Thus ordered, the procession begins and passes through the marketplace and principal streets, the owner holding forth in a kind of song the good qualities of his slaves and the high prices that have been offered for them. When any of them strikes a spectator's fancy, the line immediately stops, and a process of examination ensues which for minuteness is unequalled in any cattle market in Europe. The intending purchaser, having ascertained there is no defect in the faculties of speech, hearing, etc., that there is no disease present, and that the slave does not snore in sleeping which is counted a very great fault, next proceeds to examine the person; the mouth and the teeth are first inspected, and afterwards every part of the body in succession, not even excepting the breasts, etc., of the girls, many of whom I have seen handled in the most indecent manner in the public market by their purchasers; indeed there is every reason to believe that the slave-dealers almost universally force the young females to submit to their lust previous to their being disposed of. The slave is then made to walk or run a little way to show there is no defect about the feet; after which if the price is agreed to, they are stripped of their finery and delivered over to their future master. . . . Women and children newly born hanging at their breasts and others so old they scarcely walk, are sometimes seen dragged about in this manner. I observed they had in general a very dejected look; some groups appeared so ill fed that their bones appeared as if ready to penetrate the skin."

Africans march to market to be sold as slaves. European use of African slaves boomed in the 1400s, when the Portuguese, as well as other nations, set up trading posts along the west coast of Africa.

1508, had firsthand knowledge of West Africa from his own participation in the Portuguese voyages of discovery that took place at the end of the fifteenth century. Pacheco learned of the interior African gold trade at Lake Niger:

> At the head of this lake is a kingdom which is called Tambucutu [Timbuktu], where there is a large city of the same name close to the same lake. There also is the town of Jenne inhabited by Blacks and surrounded by a wall of mud construction, where great wealth in gold is found. There brass and copper are worth very much, as well as red and blue cloths and salt, and all is sold by weight except the cloths. And equally cloves, pepper, saffron, skeins of fine silk and sugar are greatly valued there. The trade of this region is very large.[25]

Within Akan territory, in a region known as Toom, people went to buy gold in exchange for the merchandise and slaves sold there. A strong demand for labor had arisen in the forested Akan country in the fifteenth and sixteenth centuries as farmers sought to increase the available agricultural land by clearing the forests. The Portuguese acted as middlemen, bringing slaves who could work and clear the land directly to the Akan in exchange for gold.

Because the Portuguese commanded the maritime routes, they rapidly became involved in the lucrative slave trade, moving and selling slaves up and down the West African coastline. Between 1500 and 1535 the Portuguese imported an estimated ten to twelve thousand slaves to the market city of Elmina along the Gold Coast of Africa, not far from the modern-day city of Accra. The total cost of a slave taken from the region, including purchase price, transportation, and food, was equivalent to about one-third the price of an ounce of gold. The sale price of a slave at Elmina, however, ranged from three to six ounces of gold, depending on the slave's physique. The slave traders made an enormous profit from their investment. Eventually the determined Portuguese sailors made their way around the southern tip of Africa and up the east coast, where they, and later other Europeans, discovered the well-organized Arab–East African slave-trading network.

The existence of a developed overland slave network in both West and East Africa was an important component in the development of the transatlantic slave trade. When the Portuguese, the first European voyagers to West Africa, arrived at the end of the fourteenth century, they came into contact with societies where slavery and slave trading were a part of life. The overland slave trade and the demand for slave labor within Africa predated European involvement in black slavery. However, Europeans used these existing networks to practice a new, more extensive kind of slave trading that would involve the export of millions of Africans from their continent. One hundred years after their first raid on the west coast of Africa, the Portuguese were carrying out more than three thousand slaves a year from all parts of the African continent. There were more than sixty slave markets in the Portuguese city of Lisbon, where one in ten of the city's population of one hundred thousand was a slave. With the discovery of the New World in 1492, Europeans saw the profit potential of planting sugar, tobacco, and cotton plantations there, as well as the need for labor to work these plantations. They would look to Africa, and to the slave-trading network already in place there, to fill their need.

4 Indian Slavery in the Americas

When the Mesoamerican, or Middle American, natives first encountered the Europeans, they were no strangers to the institution of slavery. Many native civilizations closely resembled the societies of Europe, Africa, and the Middle East, with despotic ruling classes at the top and serfs and slaves at the bottom. Among the most advanced early civilizations in Mexico and Central America were those of the Maya and Aztec, who occupied lands referred to as Mesoamerica. This term signifies those areas of Mexico and Central America where advanced civilizations developed before Columbus arrived in the New World in 1492. These civilizations included the Olmec, Zapotec, Maya, Teotihuacan, Toltec, Mixtec, and Aztec, all of which shared similar cultural and religious traits. Each society had extensive agricultural developments and a complex religious structure. Slavery, while not always vital to the economies, was common.

Aztec Slavery

Aztecs had many of the same sources for acquiring slaves as other cultures: prisoners of war, slaving raids, criminals, debtors, and the poor selling their families into bondage. Individuals caught stealing might be placed in slavery to the person from whom they stole. Those with gambling debts could become slaves. Those who committed homicide would either be enslaved or killed. The most common reasons for becoming a slave were extreme poverty or inability to pay taxes to the empire. Impoverished people could also apply for slave status and voluntarily place themselves in the service of another in exchange for basic food, clothing, and shelter.

The Aztec capital. Subjects in the Aztec Empire were required to pay taxes to the ruler. Those who could not afford the taxes often became slaves.

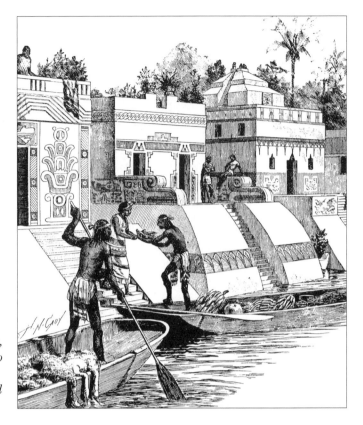

Slaves were used to transport goods, like these boatloads of fruit and animal skins, from outlying areas of the Aztec Empire to the capital. In Aztec society, slaves owed labor to their masters, but were not owned by them.

Slaves, called *tlacotin* in Aztec society, were the lowest social class. Yet they were not mistreated and were fed, housed, and clothed by their masters. Aztec slaves owed their labor to another person but were not themselves owned by those they served. This was an important distinction between Aztec slavery and the later enslavement of Aztecs by the Spanish. Aztec slaves retained many personal freedoms; they could marry as others did, and they could own property. Anyone could become a slave in Aztec society through crime or debt, and though some slaves were captives or members of other ethnic groups, many slaves were native Aztecs.

In times of hardship children were sometimes sold into slavery by their families, who could not feed them. Between 1450 and 1454 the Valley of Mexico suffered a severe famine, and many families were forced to sell their children into slavery to the people living near the Gulf of Mexico. In exchange for their children's labor, the families received maize grown on the humid coast, which had not been affected by the famine. A family that wished to buy a child back would have to pay the owner for the cost of the child's maintenance during the time of enslavement. Rather than being permanent, slavery was considered a temporary state by the Aztecs, who regarded enslavement as the result of being born under an unlucky sign. Slavery was a reversible condition.

The growing noble class in Aztec society demanded more and more slaves to serve in their households. Since the Aztecs lacked pack animals, slaves worked for the state as porters, carrying the vast quantities of food, merchandise, and taxes that reached the capital each year from all parts of the empire. The wealthiest Aztec merchants were those who dealt in slaves; they often traveled to all corners of the empire. At the time of the Spanish conquest, the buying and selling of slaves was a lucrative business throughout the Aztec Empire. The Spanish chronicler Bernal Díaz del Castillo wrote of the Aztec traders: "They bring as many slaves to be sold in that market [Tlatelolco] as the Portuguese bring Negroes from Guinea."[26] At the Aztec slave markets, male and female slaves would wear collars attached to long poles that were designed to prevent them from escaping.

Slaves who were disobedient were given three chances, under three different masters, to correct their behavior. If they did not, they would be sold as sacrificial victims. A unique custom also gave slaves a potential pathway to freedom: If slaves ran away from the marketplace where they were being sold, only their master or master's son could chase after them, and if the slave made it to the *tlatoani*'s, or ruler's, palace without being caught, they became free. This custom was strictly enforced, according to author Lois Warburton: "If in the marketplace a slave was in flight from his master and the master after him, should anyone get in the way [of this slave], grab him, obstruct his way, that person became a slave, and the slave was freed."[27]

There were other methods of gaining freedom. Because slaves sometimes held important positions, they could acquire money with which to buy their freedom. A slave could also gain freedom by marrying his or her owner, trading places with an unenslaved relative, and upon the death of the owner.

Human Sacrifice

Aztec religious ceremonies sometimes involved human sacrifice, and in many cases slaves were used in sacrificial ceremonies. The offering of fresh blood was considered a profound religious act. The extraction of the heart, a practice unique to Mesoamerican civilization, was the most common form of sacrifice. Heart extraction was also prevalent among the Maya. Without blood and human hearts, both the Aztec and the Maya believed the sun would stop shining. The Spanish conquistador, or conqueror, Cortés estimated that the Aztecs killed at least fifty people at each temple annually, which would mean that twenty thousand people were sacrificed in the Aztec Empire each year. Debtor slaves who caused trouble, and foreign slaves—usually adult males—frequently filled the sacrificial function. People captured in warfare were at the bottom of the social levels, and these people were often sent to capital cities as tribute, or gifts of respect. As sacrificial victims, they lost their right to life and became the property of the gods.

Other sacrificial victims were especially chosen from among Aztec youth, who might spend as much as a year preparing for the rituals in which they would be sacrificed. To be chosen from among the ranks for a special offering to the gods was a great honor. In an attempt to end the cycle of famine in the 1450s,

An Aztec priest holds up a dripping heart torn from a live victim's chest. The Aztecs usually used slaves for their ritual sacrifices, which they believed appeased the gods and kept the sun from failing.

priests appeased the gods with fresh blood, sacrificing hundreds of people each year.

The Maya

Around 500 B.C. the Maya emerged as a civilization characterized by monumental architecture, elaborate artwork, busy trade networks, systems of writing and mathematics, a calendar, a vast body of astrological knowledge, and a powerful noble class that controlled large cities. Mayan domains encompassed 125,000 square miles, from the present-day Pacific coast of Guatemala and El Salvador to the Yucatán Peninsula.

Like the Aztecs, the Maya made slaves of captives taken in battle, orphans, debtors, and individuals convicted of crimes. Prisoners of elite status were often reserved for sacrifices, while commoners would be made slaves. Slavery was hereditary: The children of Mayan slaves would automatically become slaves. Although debtors who were enslaved sometimes purchased their freedom, or relatives occasionally bought a slave's freedom, most slaves spent their whole lives in service as laborers, domestic servants, or farmers.

Slaves performed hard manual labor for well-to-do households. They carried merchandise on their backs, paddled canoes, ground the maize meal, gathered supplies, and fanned flies from their owners. The slaves of an important personage who died might be killed and buried with the owner to assist in the next life. This ritual sacrifice for the dead was common in many cultures.

The Maya often used slaves in religious ceremonies that involved human sacrifice. Children were often preferred for these sacrifices because of their innocence, according to Charles Gallenkamp in *Maya: The Riddle and Rediscovery of a Lost Civilization*. "If necessary," he writes, "they were sometimes abducted or even purchased from neighboring cities, the usual price being from five to ten stone beads per child."[28] The Maya practiced ritual sacrifice for, like their Mesoamerican cousins the Aztecs, they believed that human blood was essential to sustain the gods.

North American Indians

Many Indian nations practiced slavery. Among the native groups of the Pacific Northwest, who divided society into slaves, commoners, and elites, the ownership

Mayan Sacrificial Rites

Like the Aztecs, their Mesoamerican cousins, the Maya practiced human sacrifice as an offering to their gods. In Maya: The Riddle and Rediscovery of a Lost Civilization, *Charles Gallenkamp describes the use of sacrifice in Mayan culture.*

"Sacrifices played a vital part in Maya ritualism. Animals such as iguanas, crocodiles, turtles, dogs, peccaries, jaguars, and turkeys were occasionally sacrificed; . . . these offerings involved either whole animals—alive, freshly killed, or cooked—or in some cases only their hearts. But the supreme sacrifice was human life itself, and all too frequently humans were consigned to be slaughtered in the course of elaborate rituals. Such scenes are clearly depicted in sculpture, ceramics, and murals, and this gruesome practice grew out of the conviction that blood was essential to sustain the gods. Victims for these rites were provided by slaves, captured enemy soldiers, bastards, criminals, or orphans, and included adults and children of both sexes. . . . During a ritual known as the 'arrow sacrifice,' the victim— stripped and painted blue—was tied to a stake amid a group of dancers armed with bows and arrows. Upon a signal from a priest, each dancer passed in front of him, shooting at his heart until they made his whole chest like a hedgehog full of arrows."

of slaves was commonplace. The best-documented native slave-owning societies were the Klamath, Chinook, Nootka, Clatsop, and Yurok. Among these groups, slaves provided a means of displaying wealth and social status. In 1901 Silas B. Smith, who had a white father and a Clatsop mother, said of northwest coast slavery: "Almost every leading family held from one to half a dozen slaves, and some of the chiefs had even more."[29]

The Nootka of Vancouver Island acquired slaves by raiding and trading. In the wealthiest villages as many as a third of the population were slaves. One Nootka chief in the early 1800s had nearly fifty male and female slaves, according to white American John Jewitt, who was taken captive by the Nootka and lived among them from 1802 to 1806. The Nootka kept both male and female slaves, who performed menial tasks.

The Chinook of the lower Columbia River region, who were renowned slave traders, possessed more slaves per capita than any of the other surrounding tribes. Chinook slaves lived in their masters' houses. Females carried water and cut wood, and males built and repaired houses, caught fish, preserved foods, and paddled their masters' canoes. Slaves were used as wedding gifts and as a means of paying debts. But the lives of slaves were uncertain, according to historians Robert H. Ruby and John A. Brown:

A scene from the Mayan Tablet of the Slaves. Wealthy Mayans used slaves for domestic work such as paddling canoes, grinding maize, and carrying goods, but slaves also did agricultural work or were used in ritual sacrifices.

Nootka Slaves

John K. Jewitt was taken captive by the Nootka Indians from 1802 to 1806, and he later recorded the customs and traditions of these people, including their practice of slavery, in The Northwest Coast Adventure of Captain John K. Jewitt, *edited by Alice W. Shurcliff and Sarah Shurcliff Ingelfinger.*

"Their slaves, as I have observed, form their most valuable species of property. These are of both sexes, being either captives taken by themselves in war, or purchased from the neighboring tribes, and who reside in the same house, forming as it were a part of the family, are usually kindly treated, eat of the same food, and live as well as their masters. They are compelled however at times to labor severely, as not only all the menial offices are performed by them, such as bringing water, cutting wood, and a variety of others, but they are obliged to make the canoes, to assist in building and repairing the houses, to supply their masters with fish, and to attend them to war and to fight for them.

None but the king and chiefs have slaves, the common people being prevented from holding them either from their inability to purchase them, or as I am the rather inclined to think from its being considered the privilege of the former alone to have them, especially as all those made prisoners in war belong either to the king or the chiefs, who have captured them, each one holding such as have been taken by himself or his slaves. There is probably however some little distinction in favor of the king, who is always the commander of the expedition, as [Chief] Maquina had nearly fifty, male and female, in his house, a number constituting about one half of its inhabitants, comprehending [including] those obtained by war and purchase, whereas none of the other chiefs had more than twelve.

The females are employed principally in manufacturing cloth, in cooking, collecting berries, etc., and with regard to food and living in general have not a much harder lot than their mistresses, the principal difference consisting, in these poor unfortunate creatures being considered as free to any one, their masters prostituting them whenever they think proper for the purpose of gain. In this way many of them are brought on board the ships and offered to the crews."

Native Americans gather around their leader. In some Native American societies, chiefs and prominent families owned slaves, which were acquired in raids and trading.

In sickness and in health, their lot was indeed harsh. In their masters' rigid dining codes, for example, they were forced to eat meals often thrown to them and were denied nourishment for a day or two for failure to clean a dish. When incapacitated, as they often were by forced unhealthful eating practices, they were left to perish, often in inclement weather against which their inferior clothing offered little protection. Seldom did medicine men conjure evil spirits from their sick

bodies, and when they died other slaves threw their bodies to the wild animals, into the river, or into coverless pits. In some instances they were tied to their owners' sepulchers [tombs] and left to starve to death to serve their masters in the other world.[30]

Rank and social position were dominant features of Chinook society. Within the social levels, the offspring of those married to slaves became slaves. Orphans of freemen could also become slaves. Rarely were slaves able to purchase their freedom, and even after they were free, they would still be considered inferior.

Slaves in the Pacific Northwest, like those elsewhere, were acquired through intertribal wars and by raiding. Slaves could be bought and sold within a tribe or to other tribes. Groups such as the Chinook and Nootka prospered by raiding other tribes and swapping their captives for skins, furs, weapons, or polished shell beads for wampum. They goaded other tribes into attacking weaker groups, then bought the prisoners, loaded them into forty-foot canoes, and paddled up and down the coast selling them.

After the arrival of Europeans in America, slaves were often offered to white settlers in exchange for furs and guns. Many Americans founded fortunes on the fur trade along the northwest coast. According to Captain Samuel Hill of the Boston ship *Otter*, a northern Vancouver Island chief brought aboard a ten-year-old boy slave, who was traded for "fifteen clamons [eel-skin body coverings], four otter skins, and two blankets."[31] Like the European traders in Africa, American traders found they could purchase slaves from the Indians and make a profit by trading them to other native groups. In some cases unscrupulous ships' crews captured Indians, rather than trade for them, and then they made an even larger profit when they traded their captives for the skins and furs they sought.

Colonists in New England also captured Indians and either enslaved them or sold them into slavery, in some cases exchanging them for black slaves. Led by Wampanoag chief Philip, an Indian rebellion against the colonists, known as King Philip's War (1675–1676), took the lives of one-tenth of all the adult white males in Massachusetts. But the white settlers triumphed after the coalition of warring tribes ran out of food and ammunition. Following the war, hundreds of surviving Nipmuck, Wampanoag, and Narraganset Indians were captured by the whites and sold into slavery in the West Indies. Their going price was about thirty shillings each, not a very large sum at the time.

This maneuver not only helped the colonists rid themselves of Indians, it also provided them with a profit and the opportunity to purchase African slaves. John Winthrop, governor of the Massachusetts Bay Colony, was encouraged to make war on the Indians with the goal of trading them for Africans, who were then referred to as West Indian Moores, probably from the Portuguese word *Mouro*. The following

A chief tells his tribe of the arrival of Europeans in ships. The indigenous slavery in America fit in with the Europeans' enterprising plans; they grew rich trading Native American slaves and furs.

The colonists' enslavement of Native Americans often resulted in battle. One such conflict, King Philip's War, brought heavy losses for the settlers but eventual defeat for the natives.

is a proposal from Winthrop's brother-in-law, who hoped a "just war" against the Narraganset Indians would provide an opportunity to acquire some of these Moores:

> For I do not see how we can thrive until we get into a stock of slaves sufficient to do all our business, for our children's children will hardly see this great continent filled with people, so that our servants will still desire freedom to plant for themselves, and not stay but for very great wages. . . . I suppose you know very well how we shall maintain 20 Moores cheaper than one English servant.[32]

Indians were also taken captive by settlers in western America. In California from 1852 to 1867, the years following the gold rush, between three and four thousand Indian children were taken captive by settlers. The settlers sold the children to Indians and to other settlers, who used them as servants and laborers.

The arrival of Europeans in the Americas signaled a change in the pattern of slave trading in North, Central, and South America. Many Indians began selling slaves to the Europeans, rather than to each other, and by so doing they contributed to the creation of settler economies based on slave labor.

Chapter

5 Europeans Enslave Indians and Africans in the Caribbean and South America

The Caribbean peoples Columbus encountered in 1492 when he landed on the island now known as Hispaniola were unarmed, mild mannered, generous, and eager to please. He called them *los Indios*, or Indians, and put five hundred Indians on four ships and sent them to Spain. Two hundred died on the way. The rest, sick, confused, and unaccustomed to their new climate, soon died.

Other Europeans soon followed Columbus to the New World. They saw the profit potential in planting sugar, tobacco, and cotton plantations on the tropical Caribbean islands. They came upon gold mines near the coast of what is now Brazil. At first the Europeans thought the native peoples would provide all the labor they needed. The Spanish forced Mesoamerican Indians into slavery, making them work in a feudal system known as the *encomienda*. The Indians were transplanted to estates created by the Spanish and made to work the land and pay tribute to the Spanish landowners. Those who rebelled were sold as slaves and moved elsewhere. The Spanish tried to terrorize the Indians into submission. A Spanish priest, Bartolomé de Las Casas, was appalled by his countrymen's treatment of the Indians. While serving as chaplain for some Spanish troops, Las Casas witnessed a massacre at Caonao in Cuba. The soldiers, after sharpening their swords on whetstones, slaughtered a whole village with no other stated purpose than testing the sharpness of their swords. Las Casas recounted the event in his *History of the Indies:*

> To see the wounds which covered the bodies of the dead and dying was a spectacle of horror and dread: indeed, since the devil, who inspired the Spaniards, furnished them with these whetstones with which they sharpened their swords, on the morning of that very day, in the bed of the stream where they broke their fast, everywhere where they wielded their weapons upon these stark naked bodies and this delicate flesh, they cut a man in half with quite a single blow.[33]

Las Casas blamed the behavior of the Spanish on their desire for instant wealth: "I do not say that they want to kill them [the Indians] directly, from the hate they bear them, they kill them because they want to be rich and have much gold, which is their whole aim, through the toil and sweat of the afflicted and unhappy."[34] For their part, the Indians did not want to work as miners or farmers. Many preferred not to live as slaves and seemed to will themselves to die. European diseases also decimated the native Indian populations, who had no natural immunity to illnesses like smallpox, measles, and influenza. Entire towns died.

For the Portuguese and Spanish plantation owners and gold and diamond mine prospectors, the use of Indian slaves in Central and South America proved to be a disaster. The Caribbean natives were not used to a captive existence nor the heavy work of the mines and plantations. As the Europeans watched the Indians die by the hundreds each day, their visions of wealth faded. They tried to lure free peasants from Europe and appealed to their governments to send convicts to work out their sentences. But these pickings were lean.

Ironically, the very man who seemed to be a sympathetic humanitarian, Las Casas, may have made a suggestion that led to the enslavement of another people.

Las Casas observed that the few Africans in Hispaniola in the early 1500s seemed to be content and productive in the hot, humid climate. Las Casas decided that blacks were better suited to the mine and plantation work. In 1513 he appealed to King Charles V of Spain to stop enslaving the Indians and grant licenses to shippers and merchants to import blacks from Africa to work in the colonies. The king agreed.

In economic terms, when the demand for any commodity increases, people will produce more of it to supply that demand. By 1540 ten thousand Africans a year were being shackled and marched to the west coast, where they were bartered to ship captains bound for the West Indies, Mexico, and South America. By the end of the sixteenth century, nine hundred thousand African slaves had landed in the Americas. During the next hundred years, another 3 million were uprooted and transported across the Atlantic. In the 1800s the slave

---

Enslavement of the Indians

This excerpt from History of the Indies, *by the sixteenth-century Spanish priest Bartolomé de Las Casas, comes from Tzvetan Todorov's book* The Conquest of America.

"Thus husbands and wives were together once every eight or ten months, and when they met they were so exhausted and depressed on both sides that they had no mind for marital intercourse, and in this way they ceased to procreate. As for the newly born, they died early because their mothers, overworked and famished, had no milk to nurse them with, and for this reason, while I was in Cuba, 7000 children died in three months. Some mothers even drowned their babies from sheer desperation, while others caused themselves to abort with certain herbs which produced stillborn children."

Spaniards force Indians to carry heavy loads. When the enslavement of Native Americans resulted in mass deaths, the Spanish imported African slaves, who were thought to be better suited to the work.

trade became the world's biggest industry. Nobody knows exactly how many—or what percentage—of Africa's population were enslaved. Estimates vary from 10 to 20 million.

The Slavery Business

Profitable businesses always attract competition. Watching the Portuguese grow rich in the slave trade inspired the Dutch, French, and English to open their own forts along the African coast. At one time in the late 1700s there were forty trading posts. Eventually the British gained the predominant position, controlling 90 percent of the slave trade.

The slave business was only one-third, although it was the essential third, of a triangle trade that produced great wealth.

The ships that carried the slaves to the Caribbean and the mainland then filled their holds with sugar, rum, molasses, spices, cotton, gold, and tobacco for the eager consumers of Europe. After selling these goods in their home ports, the traders reloaded with weapons, fabrics, wines, carpets, and whatever else the African chiefs desired in exchange for the slaves they provided. Money was rarely involved; most of the trade was by barter.

The British port of Liverpool became the capital of the industry. By 1800 ships built, manned, and outfitted in Liverpool were transporting about 90 percent of the slaves from Africa. In addition to hundreds of small businesses, which benefited from servicing the ships and sailors, British factories turned out the trade goods sought by the African chiefs. The entire city of Liverpool and a good part of the Industrial Revolution were built on

Slave trading (pictured) attracted Europeans, who viewed Africa as a prime source of profit and dotted the coast with trading posts.

formed the established pattern of local rivalries and tribal wars into wide-ranging raids with no other cause or agenda than the roundup of people to sell. A life of slavery began for most Africans with an otherwise peaceful day shattered by a raid on their village by a more powerful tribe or by a chief's private army. Former slave Olaudah Equiano, who in the 1780s and 1790s became a prominent spokesperson for the English black community, told of the day of his capture in Africa when he was eleven years old:

> One day, when all our people were gone out to their work as usual and only I and my dear sister were left to mind the house, two men and a woman got over our walls, and in a moment seized us both, and without giving us time to cry out to make resistance they stopped our mouths and ran off with us into the nearest woods.[35]

Captives would be bound or chained together and marched, sometimes for weeks, to a depot where they were turned over to a middleman. From there, often carrying heavy loads of gold and ivory, they trudged to the coastal holding forts.

At the coast they would see a ship's agent or doctor, who would look them over before closing the deal. The slaves were then branded with the ship's mark and loaded aboard. Chained together closely and forced to stay below deck in a space too low to stand, as many as half of them died before reaching land. Fearing epidemics, the captain would throw overboard any slave who showed symptoms of a contagious disease. Some slaves chose suicide by jumping into the sea during their few minutes on deck each day or by refusing to eat.

the black backs of Africans. The same was true for some of the ports of France, where everyone who owned at least one ship used it to buy and sell slaves.

On the other side of the Atlantic, buyers of the slaves prospered by selling their sugar and other harvests of the slaves' labor back to Europe. The only people who got nothing at all out of slavery were the slaves themselves and the ordinary natives in Africa who escaped the raiding parties but never tasted the luxuries enjoyed by their rulers and exploiters. In Africa the rapidly growing market for slaves trans-

Ship captains, who shared in the profits with their backers, packed the holds of their ships with up to seven hundred slaves. The slaves were fed a mush made from beans, rice, yams, and corn cooked together. In good weather they were allowed on deck to take in the fresh air, since healthy slaves commanded the highest prices upon arrival. And a doctor was usually onboard to tend to the slaves' illnesses during the two-month journey known as the Middle Passage. Olaudah Equiano described his own middle passage:

The closeness of the place and the heat of the climate, added to the number of the ship, which was so crowded that each had scarcely room to turn himself, almost suffocating us. This produced copious [plentiful] perspirations, so that the air soon became unfit for respiration from a variety of loathsome smells, and brought on a sickness among the slaves, of which many died.[36]

The slaves' white captors also died at similar, if not higher, rates because of

Panicked and confused, East African villagers scramble into boats to escape the slave raiders. Millions of Africans were forced into slavery after being taken captive in similar raids.

The Middle Passage

The transatlantic crossing was an unspeakable horror for slaves who were crowded in the holds of ships. Cleric Alonso de Sandoval of Brazil believed that one-third of the slaves usually died during the voyage. Historian William Phillips's Slavery from Roman Times to the Early Transatlantic Trade *contains the cleric's description of conditions in slave ships that arrived in Brazil in the seventeenth century.*

"They [the slaves] were so crowded, in such disgusting conditions, and so mistreated, as the very ones who transport them assure me, that they come six by six, with collars around their necks, and these same ones by two and two with fetters [chains] on their feet, in such a way that they come imprisoned from head to feet, below the deck, locked in from outside, where they see neither sun nor moon, [and] that there is no Spaniard who dares stick his head in the hatch without becoming ill, nor to remain inside for an hour without the risk of great sickness. So great is the stench, the crowding and the misery of that place. And the [only] refuge and consolation that they have in it is [that] to each [is given] once a day no more than a half bowl of uncooked corn flour or millet, which is like our rice, and with it a small jug of water and nothing else, except for much beating, much lashing, and bad words. This is that which commonly happens with the men and I well think that some of the shippers treat them with more kindness and mildness, principally in these times. . . . [Nevertheless, most] arrive turned into skeletons."

Armed traders pass through the hold of a slave ship crowded with emaciated slaves, one of whom collapses in front of them. Many slaves did not survive the Middle Passage due to beatings, starvation, and disease.

their exposure to alien African diseases. Only 10 percent of the men sent to work on English slavers lived to return. One in every four white sailors died during the Middle Passage.

Arrival

A few days before arriving at their destination, the surviving slaves were given extra food and smeared with a glossy oil to give them a healthy appearance. The arrival of a convoy of slave ships was a festive event. Sometimes an entire shipload of slaves had been prepurchased or sold to one buyer. But more often the captain would either sell his cargo at a public auction or invite what was called a scramble. First the captain separated the sick and dying and sold them as one lot to a speculator for as little as one dollar. If the rest were to be sold at auction, they were stripped naked for inspection by potential buyers.

Scrambles were wild events. The captain would put a fixed price on each category—male, female, young, old—then open the gates to the holding pen. Buyers would swarm in, grabbing and fighting over the healthiest specimens, frantically trying to keep a grip on every one they claimed, while grasping for another who met his needs. This furious activity so panicked the already trembling slaves that some of them would break loose and run half-crazed through the town, chased by a howling mob of hopeful buyers. Once bought, the slaves were then branded again, this time with their new owner's red-hot iron. In the Caribbean and South America, most of the slaves wound up in Brazil, Haiti, or Cuba. While the treat-

A trader puffs on his pipe as he presses a red-hot iron onto a slave's back. Slaves were branded with their ship's mark before leaving Africa and were branded again by their new owner.

ment of slaves varied from country to country, life on a Caribbean or South American plantation was harsh.

The Use and Treatment of Slaves

Nowhere were the idle rich more idle while growing more wealthy than the Portuguese plantation owners of Brazil. Slaves did everything for them, literally waiting on them hand and foot. Those who labored in the coffee and sugar fields put in eighteen-hour days. Their masters did not

Portuguese landowners in Brazil look over adult and child slaves. The Portuguese settlers in Brazil reaped the profits of their plantations while literally working their slaves to death.

care if the slaves worked themselves to death in a year or two; it was cheap enough to replace them. With an endless supply of slave labor, Brazilians saw no need to invest in machinery. As early as the 1550s, a visitor to Brazil remarked on the importance of slave labor: "As soon as persons who intend to live in Brazil become inhabitants of the country, however poor they may be, if each one obtains two pairs or one half-dozen slaves . . . he then has the means of sustenance."[37]

The slaves proved invaluable in another way when gold and, later, diamonds were discovered in Brazil in the sixteenth century. The Portuguese knew nothing about mining, but many of the Africans, who had come from areas of West Africa where gold was mined, knew about mining techniques. The slaves also knew about smuggling gold dust and diamonds, which they sold to raise money to buy freedom—if they lived long enough.

Many Brazilian slaves ran away to establish their own settlements in the jungles and remote hill country. Or they made their way to the cities, where, if they had a skill or a trade, they might pass themselves off as freemen. From time to time there were uprisings, but few succeeded. The slaves had been captured from so many different tribes and regions of Africa that they were unable to unite. Language and cultural differences separated them.

Haiti

In Haiti, which was settled in 1629 by a party of French adventurers who called the island San Domingo, the French planted cotton, sugar, coffee, and other crops. The island's climate and primitive living conditions did not appeal to most Europeans, and the early workforce consisted mostly of fugitives, escaped slaves, white slaves supplied by the Spaniards, and even Indians from Canada and Louisiana. Reports of Haiti's fertile soil for growing coffee and sugar drew investment interest from

French nobility, some of whom came to live on the island, bringing their lavish lifestyles with them. But for slaves on a sugar plantation, life could be harsh. Official French records support historian C. L. R. James's description of punishments given to slaves:

> There was no ingenuity that fear or a depraved imagination could devise which was not employed to break [the slaves'] spirit and satisfy the lusts and resentment of their owners and guardians—irons on the hands and feet, blocks of wood that the slaves had to drag behind them wherever they went, the tin-plate mask designed to prevent the slaves from eating the sugar cane, the iron collar. Whipping

Destroying Tradition

Diego Duran, a sixteenth-century Spanish priest who lived in Mexico from the age of six, wrote a description of the pre-Columbian world, Book of the Gods and Rites and the Ancient Calendar. *He warned other priests of the enormous task of culturally enslaving the Indians—of making them reject their religion and customs in favor of Christianity and Spanish traditions.*

"[The Indians] will never find God until the roots have been torn out, together with that which smacks of the ancestral religion. If we are trying earnestly to remove the memory of [their god] Amalech, we shall never succeed until we fully understand the ancient religion. . . . Those who with fervent zeal (though with little prudence) in the beginning burned and destroyed all the ancient Indian pictographic [picture written] documents were mistaken. They left us without a light to guide us—to the point that the Indians worship idols in our presence, and we understand nothing of what goes on in their dances, in their marketplaces, in their bathhouses, in the songs they chant (when they lament their ancient gods and lords), in their repasts [meals] and banquets; these things mean nothing to us. . . . Let [God's priest] not consider them things of little concern! If he does not fight against them, reprehend [criticize] them, showing wrath and grief over them, the natives become accustomed [to our lenience]. . . . Let [our ministers] in their laxity and negligence, in their idleness and recreation, not permit the Indians to practice even small things, such as the shearing of the children's heads, the feathering with plumes of wild fowl, nor the smearing of rubber upon their heads or on their foreheads, nor the smearing with pitch, nor the anointing with holy bitumen."

was interrupted in order to pass a piece of hot wood on the buttocks of the victim; salt, pepper, citron, cinders, aloes, and hot ashes were poured on the bleeding wounds. Mutilations were common, limbs, ears, and sometimes the private parts, to deprive them of the pleasures which they could indulge in without expense. Their masters poured burning wax on their arms and hands and shoulders, emptied the boiling cane sugar over their heads, burned them alive, roasted them on slow fires, filled them with gunpowder and blew them up with a match, buried them up to the neck and smeared their heads with sugar that the flies might devour them, fastened them near to nests of ants or wasps, made them eat their excrement, drink their urine, and lick the saliva of other slaves.[38]

Meanwhile, coffee and sugar produced enormous profits for the planters and for France, which required that all trade involving its colonies had to be done with the home country. French ships carried the slaves from Africa to Haiti, and the produce from Haiti to France; all the provisions and equipment required in Haiti had to be bought from French merchants. At one time half of all the sugar and coffee in the world came from Haiti. For one hundred years those two crops produced more profits per square mile in Haiti than any other place on earth. They also produced the most successful slave revolt in history.

Cruel treatment of slaves was common in Haiti. To exert their authority, French owners doled out humiliating punishments that often resulted in the slave's death.

By the 1780s five of every six people in Haiti were black slaves; there were five hundred thousand slaves to thirty-five thousand whites, with another thirty-five thousand free blacks and mixed races. As in most slave societies, the city slaves lived better than the plantation gangs. One city slave was François-Dominique Toussaint-Louverture, a middle-aged descendant of an African chieftain. (The chieftain had been captured in a tribal war and sold to slavers.) A man of extraordinary intelligence, Toussaint-Louverture luckily wound up in the home of a kind master, who educated him and appointed him a steward, or overseer, of his estate.

The French Revolution that toppled the monarchy in the name of liberty and equality for all roused a similar movement for more rights for the colonies. Haitian whites won the right to make their own laws, but they did not give equal rights to the free blacks and mulattoes (people of mixed black and white ancestry). The slaves, catching the freedom fever, rose up on August 14, 1791. They set fire to everything that would burn and hacked to death every white person they found. Thousands of whites fled by ship to North America. When French troops arrived to restore order, Toussaint-Louverture emerged as the slaves' leader. He organized an army and taught them how to fight. For three years they fought off the French, as well as British and Spanish forces who tried to seize the island. But the warfare devastated the once rich nation. Finally, in 1794 the French National Assembly abolished slavery in its colonies and appointed Toussaint-Louverture the official governor-general representing France.

Faced with the daunting job of restoring the island's productivity, Toussaint-

Slaves hang a white settler while other whites dangle from gallows in the background. The rebellion of 1791 in Haiti, led by an educated slave, Toussaint-Louverture, was the most successful slave revolt in history.

Louverture allowed the ten thousand remaining whites to reclaim the plantations rather than carving up the land to give each former slave a small plot to farm. He ordered the former slaves to work at their old plantations as sharecroppers. Although these policies restored much of the production, the former slaves believed Toussaint-Louverture had been too lenient with their former masters. They resented being forced to work for them again. They tried to overthrow Toussaint-Louverture, who put down the rebellion. He then wrote a constitution declaring Haiti's independence from France and abolishing slavery and all race distinctions.

Toussaint-Louverture's actions angered Napoleon, the French dictator, who sent an army in 1802 to destroy Toussaint-Louverture and reinstate slavery in Haiti. But the Haitian army wreaked more damage on Napoleon's troops than they had ever suffered in their European conquests. More than sixty thousand soldiers from both sides died under fire or from yellow fever in seven months of bloody fighting. When the French commander negotiated separate agreements with each of Toussaint-Louverture's generals, the isolated black leader was forced to sue for peace. Napoleon ordered Toussaint-Louverture sent to France, where he died in a dungeon on April 7, 1803. But Napoleon's efforts to return slavery to Haiti failed, and the islanders declared their independence on December 31, 1803.

Toussaint-Louverture was criticized by his followers for allowing remaining whites to reclaim their plantations and ordering former slaves to work on them as sharecroppers.

Cuba

The native population of Cuba had also made attempts to rise up against enslavement by their oppressors, the Spanish, but their revolts ended in massive casualties. These rebellions, combined with epidemics of disease, managed to decimate the native islanders by the middle of the sixteenth century. The Spaniards soon turned to the use of African slaves to work the rich sugar and tobacco plantations. The few white immigrants who ventured to Cuba made their fortunes and went home as fast as they could. By the end of the sixteenth century, the twenty thousand blacks far outnumbered the Spanish. The blacks were the only ones capable of doing all the skilled labor—the construc-

tion, farming, and other occupations essential to a society. In the cities many slaves were rented out by their masters. They retained a portion of their earnings, secured their own housing, entered into contracts, and edged toward the complete freedom they could purchase.

Cuba soon became a mixed population of wealthy and poor whites, free blacks, and slaves. The mix remained stable until the slave revolt in Haiti drastically curtailed coffee and sugar production on that island. The French planters who fled Haiti landed in Cuba. While Haitians bled, Cuba gradually replaced Haiti as the largest sugar producer in the world and the largest market for slaves. During the next thirty years, more than 225,000 Africans arrived. Hardly a week passed during the rest of the nineteenth century without the arrival of a slave ship. In one year an estimated 60,000 slaves were sold in the marketplace. Those who participated in the slave trade made enormous profits. One American sailor recalled the markup on slaves his ship transported to Cuba in 1835:

> I filled the place of mate and surgeon on a voyage when she sailed with 250 full-grown men and a hundred boys and girls, for the Cuban market. The cargo was consigned to my old friend Gomez and rated A-1. By actual calculation the average cost per head of the 350 blacks was $16, and in Havana the market average was $360, yielding a net profit, if safely delivered, of $120,400 for the cargo, from

which should be deducted $20,000 as the average cost of the clipper's round trip, including commissions. This would mark her earnings for the voyage, as about $100,000. Such were the enormous profits of the slave trade in 1835. After that, with greater risks, the average of successful voyages ran higher still.[39]

The heavy labor demands of the sugar industry transformed Cuba from a relatively benign culture of semi-free city slaves and small farmers into a brutal slave-gang society. A former slave, Esteban Montejo, told of the living conditions:

> There were barracoons [barracks housing up to 200 slaves] of wood and barracoons of masonry with tiled roofs. Both types had mud floors and were dirty as hell. And there was no modern ventilation there. Just a hole

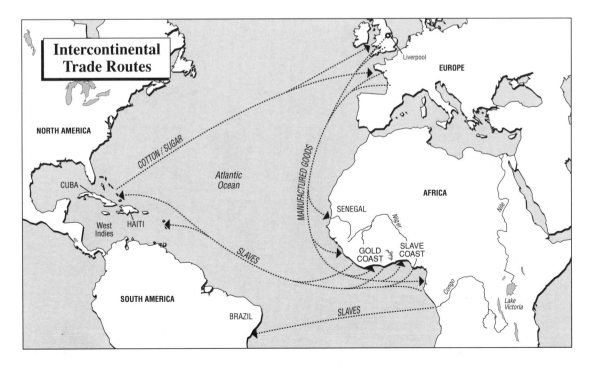

in the wall or a small barred window. The result was that the place swarmed with fleas and ticks, which made the inmates ill with infections and evil spells, for those ticks were witches. . . . As the rooms were so small the slaves relieved themselves in a so-called toilet standing in one corner of the barracoon. Everybody used it.[40]

The need for a constant flow of new slaves was made greater by three factors. The death rate among slaves on the sugar plantations was high, as they worked long hours and lived in squalid conditions. Second, slaves sometimes ran away and hid in the forests and hills of Cuba, where they mixed with free blacks. They settled in villages where they farmed, herded cattle, and traded with town dwellers and wan-

dering renegades and smugglers. Third, Cuba had liberal manumission laws. Encouraged by a strong Catholic Church, which accepted free blacks and slaves equally in rites and ceremonies, the law enabled slaves to contract for their freedom on an installment plan. A court set the price and the payments. Using his savings from hiring out as a skilled tradesman or from selling crops raised on a small plot of land allotted to him, a slave could aspire to a freedom that guaranteed him all the rights and privileges of any other citizen.

In 1807 Britain and the United States outlawed the slave trade, and the closing of the British and U.S. markets deflected the slave trade to Cuba and Brazil, where as late as 1850 more than fifty thousand slaves a year were imported. Abolitionist

Cuba's sugar production boomed after the Haitian rebellion. The sugar plantations required a steady flow of slave labor (pictured), and consequently Cuba became the world's largest importer of slaves.

A slave stands on display at an auction. Brazilian and Portuguese colonies gradually improved the treatment of slaves as well as the standard of living and rights of freed slaves.

movements in Britain and the United States helped to create a worldwide reaction against slavery, which pressured Cuba and Brazil into the process of abolition.

The Portuguese and Spanish had gradually humanized the slave system in the Americas. When a group of slave owners proposed the cutting of the Achilles tendons, which join leg muscles to heel bones, of captured runaway slaves, the Portuguese government rejected the idea. By 1784 the Spanish Empire had abolished the branding of slaves. Portuguese law required slaves to be baptized into the Roman Catholic Church within a year of their arrival. The church encouraged manumission, and when slaves became free, they enjoyed a status equal to free whites, with all the same rights and opportunities. A Portuguese royal decree of May 31, 1789, which codified the legislation on Negro slave matters, strictly regulated an owner's freedom to mete out punishments and stipulated that slaves were to be fed and clothed decently.

By 1822 Brazil had declared its independence from Portugal, and in 1850 transatlantic slave shipments were outlawed by the Brazilian government under pressure from British naval forces. The free-birth law passed in Brazil in 1871 deprived the slave system of its only other means of perpetuating itself, and in the 1880s emancipation finally came to both Brazil and Cuba. Since free blacks, who had gradually come to outnumber slaves in Cuba, had long formed the majority of the skilled industrial workers in the economy, they enjoyed a standard of living far above that of the freed blacks of North America at the end of the nineteenth century.

Chapter

6 Slavery in the American Colonies and the United States

Two separate economies developed in northern and southern colonial America. In the North, where small farms and mills predominated, slaveholdings were small, and most slaves were domestic servants in the coastal cities. In the South a cash-crop economy based on plantation agriculture developed. A large labor force was needed to work the cotton, indigo, and tobacco plantations. Over the years, as the North grew more industrialized and the South remained tied to a cash-crop economy fueled by slave labor, the differences between the northern and southern economies would prompt the South to secede, a move that would lead to battle and bloodshed.

The North was instrumental in the development of the southern economy because of its dominance in the slave trade that brought African labor to the colonies. Despite the sparse use of slaves in New England, profits from the slave trade provided the foundations on which the region's most powerful and prestigious families were built. The ports of Massachusetts, Rhode Island, and Connecticut built the slave ships and sailed them, at one time carrying 90 percent of the slave cargoes to America.

The transatlantic slave trade between Africa and North America lasted less than 170 years, although slavery existed in the colonies and the new United States before

While the industrialized northern United States used few slaves, the large plantations of the South depended upon slave labor to tend the crops, which included cotton (pictured), indigo, and tobacco.

the 1640s and after 1807. Between 1492 and 1770 more Africans than Europeans came to the New World, but only 4.5 percent of them were imported into the region that later became the United States. Most were carried to the Caribbean and to South America. In 1619 the first Africans were brought to the Chesapeake Bay area of colonial Virginia.

The invention of the cotton gin and spinning and weaving machines at the end of the eighteenth century sealed the fate of thousands of Africans. Spinning and weaving machines could produce cotton cloth at low cost. The cotton gin, which could mechanically separate the seeds from the cotton bolls, was able to work fifty times faster than a person, and it helped small farms grow rapidly into huge plantations that required thousands of cheap laborers to produce a raw cotton supply for the textile mills. Southern planters could not keep up with the demand from the mills of the North and England. Planters moved west into Alabama, Mississippi, Louisiana, Texas—all the way to California—to expand their plantations. By the 1860s southern plantations were producing 75 percent of the world's cotton. They needed not only more land, but more hands for the backbreaking work. The slave traders of New England and the native chiefs of Africa provided the bodies.

The New England Triangle Trade

The profit potential of the so-called New England triangle trade was enormous. As early as the 1700s New Englanders recog-

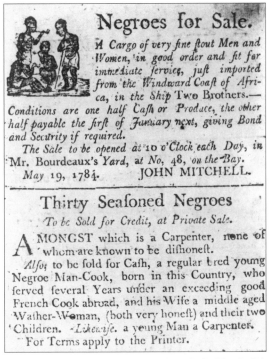

An advertisement for slaves. Although the North did not use much slave labor, New England merchants were heavily involved in the slave trade.

nized the importance of this trade. New England merchants used rum to purchase slaves on the West African coast, who would then be traded in the South, the Caribbean, or South America, usually for molasses, which would be used to make more rum. Thus the trade was self-perpetuating. The following description comes from a letter written by a New Englander who resettled in the West Indies:

> If you go to Barbados, you will see a flourishing island, many able men. I believe they have bought this year no less than a thousand negroes, and the more they buy, the better able they are to buy, for in a year and a half they will earn (with God's blessing) as much as they cost.[41]

The following letter from James De Wolf of Bristol, Rhode Island, to Captain Jonathan Dennison—who was to sail De Wolf's ship, the *Ann*, to Africa, South America, and back to Rhode Island—reveals how the shippers made their money:

Sir, Your having engaged me to go on a Voyage to Africa in my ship *Ann*, my Instructions are that you proceed with all possible Dispatch direct to Cape Coast, and make Trade at the Place and its Vicinity, and purchase as many good healthy young Slaves as may be in your power to purchase, by bartering away your present cargo with the Natives; and after completing your Business in Africa, you will proceed to Monte Video in South America, and there dispose of your slaves, and purchase a return cargo of ox hides and dried beef and some tallow and other produce of that country, such as you may judge will pay a handsome profit, and after completing your Business there, you will return home to this Port with all possible Dispatch.[42]

Slavery and the Constitution

Americans today have a difficult time understanding how the early Americans justified slavery with the Declaration of Independence and its message that "All men are created equal." "All men," however, did not include slaves. Slaves were property to early Americans, not people. They had no rights. A runaway slave was like a horse or a cow, to be returned to its rightful owner. Although some slaveholders wrestled with the ethics of slavery, they continued to sanction it.

Many of the early American statesmen believed that slavery was a dying institution, and they hoped that it would end sooner rather than later. In a 1786 letter to a fellow Virginian, George Washington wrote: "I never mean (unless some peculiar circumstance compel me to it) to possess another slave by purchase; it being among my first wishes to see some plan adopted, by which slavery in this country may be abolished by slow, sure, and imperceptible degrees."[43]

Some politicians who had experience with slavery were uncomfortable with the practice because they had observed the power dynamic that was created between a master and a slave. Thomas Jefferson, a Virginia native and a slaveholder himself, wrote:

The whole commerce between master and slave is a perpetual exercise of the most boisterous passions, the most unremitting despotism on the one part, and degrading submissions on the other. Our children see this, and learn to imitate it, and daily exercised in tyranny, cannot but be stamped by it with odious peculiarities.[44]

When the Continental Congress met in 1787 to write a constitution for the new nation, many of the states wanted to abolish slavery. The northern states had little need for slaves, and many people had come to despise the cruelties of the transatlantic slave trade. Seven northern states had outlawed slavery by 1787. But since the plantation economies of the southern states depended on slave labor, abolition was unthinkable to most southerners. For them the crucial issue was

Slave and White Children at Play

In his article "The Play of Slave Children in the Plantation Communities of the Old South," in Journal of Sport History, *Professor David Wiggins explores the culture and pastimes of young slaves.*

"Slave children held a rather precarious position in the plantation community. For six days a week, while their parents were in the fields toiling under the hot sun or attending to chores in the 'big house,' slave children were generally left alone to raise one another. Exempted from routine labor until sometimes as late as fourteen or fifteen years old, a certain portion of the slave child's early life was spent in nurturing those younger than themselves and performing such chores as carrying water to the field hands, cleaning up the yards, fetching wood, tending the family garden, and feeding the livestock. The slave children's existence, however, was not all work and no play. . . .

Much of the leisure time of slave and white children was spent in getting into mischief and helping each other out of difficult situations. Hand in hand they would go about pilfering the plantation hen house and performing no small amount of reciprocal trading. There are also numerous examples of white children helping their slave playmates avoid punishments or assisting them in a variety of subtle ways. 'Me and young master had the good times,' recalled Jack Cauthern of Texas. 'He was nigh my age and we'd steal chickens from old Miss and go down in the orchard and barbecue 'em.' Matilda Daniel said they sure did some 'devilish' things on her Alabama plantation. 'We hid red pepper in old Black Bob's chewin' bacca, an' you ought to seed de faces he made. Den we tuken a skunk dat us little white an' black debils katched an' turn him loose in de slave quarters.' "

This illustration depicts slave and white children playing together.

whether slaves would count as people in the population tallies that determined political representation. The constitutional delegates were able to reach a compromise on the issues of slavery and representation. They decided that for the purposes of representation, each slave would count as three-fifths of a person. Furthermore, individual states would be allowed to phase out slavery in their own time and their own ways—and the African slave trade could continue for twenty more years, until 1807. Under a fugitive-slave clause, runaway slaves would have to be returned to their owners even if they reached free states. The Constitution also promised that the government would assist in putting down slave revolts.

Although fewer than 500,000 of the 30 million slaves kidnapped from Africa had entered North American ports, generations of breeding had raised their number in the United States to 4 million by 1860. Slaves outnumbered free whites in Mississippi and South Carolina. The 1830 U.S. census reported that 3,777 black families also owned slaves, including one black plantation owner who held a hundred. Between the trading centers of Alexandria, Virginia, in the north and New Orleans, Louisiana, in the south, a network of slave dealers, transporters, runaway-slave catchers, and kidnappers of free blacks prospered. Every southern city had a slave market. It included an auction block and a holding pen, which could be anything from a converted stable to a large, secure building housing the human merchandise for inspection by bidders. The sellers and dealers were many; the buyers were few. Most families never owned a slave. They were expensive: Two sound slaves were worth more than many a man's land and house and everything in it. Half of those who did own slaves had fewer than five. Only a few thousand large plantation owners bought most of the slaves to work in the cotton-producing states.

Slave Life on a Southern Plantation

The vast holdings of a handful of the wealthiest and most powerful plantation owners required overseers to manage them for the absentee owners. Each overseer was judged by the amount of cotton he could make the plantation produce. That was all that mattered, and it left no room for humanitarian feelings. Apart from the inevitable uncalled-for brutality and torture inflicted by some depraved or drunken overseers, whippings and brandings became routine punishments for the slightest infractions of the rules. The failure to pick the daily quota of cotton brought the lash cutting into a slave's back. Runaways felt the red-hot branding iron and the whip when they were caught. Forbidden to marry, but often paired off at the whim of the master, slaves were often denied any form of family life. Children born to slaves could be sold, brothers and sisters separated, never to meet again.

Southern slaves enjoyed few material comforts. Their diet was plain, usually cornmeal, pork fat, molasses, and sometimes coffee. Many masters allowed their slaves to keep gardens, where they often grew sweet potatoes and greens. Still, many slaves suffered the effects of dietary-deficiency diseases like pellagra, which is

A slave woman's son is pried from her grasp to be led off with his new owner. Once slaves were parted from spouses, children, or other family members, they may have never seen each other again.

the result of a lack of niacin and protein. Slaves were often crowded into tiny cabins. Lack of sanitation led to the spread of disease. Slave quarters were usually crude, one-room structures with dirt floors and log walls packed with mud to keep out the weather. Servants in the more modest households lived in dormitory-like quarters in back of the main house.

On large plantations slaves would begin work before dawn and not finish until well after sunset. Slaves who worked on tobacco plantations had to pick the sticky, often smelly, tobacco leaves, and if they failed to remove all the tobacco worms, they could be made to eat them in front of their master. Women did heavy fieldwork alongside men, often during pregnancy. Old people took care of slave children, and ginned, carded, and spun cotton. Slave children had to carry water to the fields, gather kindling for the fire, and sweep the yards.

The domestic servants in the plantation houses led a better life. They ate the leftovers from the master's table and wore the discarded clothes. Indeed, a well-dressed butler and footman were a credit to his master. Although household slaves were better off, they too could be cruelly punished for trivial reasons. Mrs. Nancy Howard, an escaped slave who later lived in Canada, recounted her experience:

When you told them the truth, they whip you to make you lie. I have taken more lashes for this, than for any other thing, because I would not lie. . . . I was frequently punished with raw hides, was hit with tongs and pokers and any thing. I used when I went out, to look up at the sky, and say, "Blessed

Slave quarters on plantations usually consisted of log huts with dirt floors. The conditions were crowded and unsanitary, and disease was rampant.

Lord, oh, do take me out of this." It seemed to me I could not bear another lick. I can't forget it. I sometimes dream that I am pursued, and when I wake, I am scared almost to death.[45]

In the cities slaves who were skilled tradesmen enjoyed some measure of freedom, especially those who were rented out and lived apart from the master. By the 1850s about two hundred thousand slaves, most of them rented out by the year, worked in heavy industries in the cities. For them, kind treatment and rewards replaced the whip, because a resentful slave could ruin a business by sabotaging expensive machinery. Production above the daily quota brought cash bonuses paid directly to the slaves. They could save money in bank accounts or spend it on fine clothes and good food. In addition, they learned valuable technological skills. When freedom came, and the post–Civil War climate was not friendly to freed

blacks, many of them remained at their same jobs.

African slaves in America responded to their plight in a variety of ways. Some sought consolation in religion and the promise of a better life after death. Others rebelled against their masters in subtle ways, by breaking tools, pretending to be sick, or deliberately breaking one of their own arms or legs to avoid the hard labor and to cripple the productivity of their master's plantation.

Runaways and Revolts

Slaves who ran away faced torture, the lash, branding, or the selling of their children if they were caught. Free states were hundreds of miles away from the plantations of the deep South. Even if a slave made it to a free state, slave catchers were everywhere, hungry for the rewards of returning a runaway slave. But there were helping hands for those slaves lucky enough to reach them. Free blacks and white sympathizers developed a network of safe havens in their homes and barns between the middle states and Canada. The chain came to be known as the Underground Railroad. Traveling at night from one station to another, thousands of runaways reached freedom in the North and across the Canadian border. Harriet Tubman, an African-American woman and an escaped slave herself, was one of the most heroic conductors of the railroad. Tubman risked her life and freedom many times by going into the southern states and guiding escaped slaves to the safe havens.

Some slaves plotted armed uprisings, which offered a chance for revenge more than escape. No one knows how many small revolts took place, as plantation owners suppressed the news of uprisings so that other slaves would not be infected with the fervor. Slaves could be hanged solely on rumors of being rebellious inciters. Others died when fellow conspirators betrayed them.

The most notable rebellion was led by Nat Turner, a slave carpenter in Virginia who had also been a preacher. The Turner uprising included one hundred slaves. In the early morning of August 22, 1831, Turner led a band of rebels from house to house in Southampton County, Virginia, killing whites and severing their limbs with axes and guns. The uprising was quelled within forty-eight hours, but not before Turner's band had murdered fifty-eight white people, many of them children. Turner eluded capture for several weeks, and when he and approximately two

Well-dressed slaves line up before the auction. Slaves who worked in a house could wear the owner's old clothing, or if the slave was a tradesman, he could be rented out and earn money to buy his own clothes.

hundred other blacks lost their lives as a result of the rebellion, his name became a symbol for black hopes and white fears. Coinciding with the Turner rebellion was the nullification crisis of 1831, a confrontation sparked by South Carolina's opposition to federal taxation policy and by the larger fear that the federal government might someday abolish slavery. Led by U.S. vice president John C. Calhoun, South Carolina politicians fought for the preservation of slavery by demanding state sovereignty, the right to self-government without federal interference.

American antislavery sentiment grew in the 1850s as the abolitionist movement gained popular support, in part because of widespread disapproval of and resistance to the fugitive slave law. Passed in 1850, the law required federal marshals to arrest any black as a fugitive slave if any white person claimed him as a runaway. Since the marshal earned a fee for

doing so and suffered a fine for not doing so, many a free black was sold into slavery on the word of a lying white man. Anyone who helped a runaway faced a prison term or fine. In 1857 the U.S. Supreme Court ruled in the *Dred Scott* case that an escaped slave did not gain freedom just by reaching a free, nonslave state. The slave remained the property of his master. However, some states and many individuals refused to comply with this ruling.

As the nation pushed westward, the debate over slavery became more heated. Political leaders who longed for an end to slavery opposed its expansion into the new states and territories. The admission of Missouri into the Union in 1820 divided the nation into proslavery and antislavery factions that split along geographic—southern and northern—lines. Some of the aging founders of the nation, including Thomas Jefferson and James

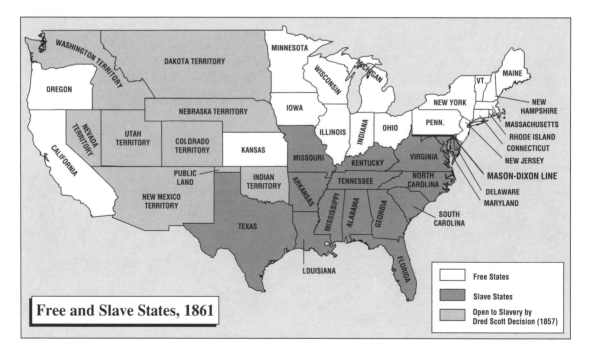

Free and Slave States, 1861

Free States

Slave States

Open to Slavery by
Dred Scott Decision (1857)

Runaway slaves trek on a rainy night to an Undergound Railroad depot. Thousands of slaves gained freedom by following the Underground Railroad to the northern United States and Canada.

Madison, deplored the divisiveness of the slavery issue. "All these perplexities," Madison wrote, "develop more and more, the dreadful fruitfulness of the original sin of the African trade."[46] The eighty-one-year-old Jefferson, calling slavery "a blot in our moral history," confessed that he saw no easy solution to the problem:

> I shall not live to see it, but those who come after us will be wiser than we are, for light is spreading and man improving. To that advancement I look, and to the dispensations [revealed commands] of an all-wise and all-powerful providence [divine guidance] to devise the means of effecting what is right.[47]

The Abolitionists

Since the 1840s free blacks and whites from New England down to the South had joined the fight for the abolition of slavery. They held public meetings, published

newspapers, aided the Underground Railroad, and petitioned state legislatures and Congress to end slavery. In 1854 about fifty abolitionists met at a schoolhouse in Ripon, Wisconsin, to organize and work for a political solution. This group grew into the Republican Party.

After leading a slave rebellion in which fifty-eight white people were killed, Nat Turner is apprehended and held at gunpoint.

The Mixing of Races

Mary Boykin Chesnut, a Confederate woman from Charleston, South Carolina, kept a diary in which she recorded her thoughts on slavery and the mixing of the races. The following excerpt is quoted in Roll Jordan Roll: The World the Slaves Made *by Eugene Genovese.*

"(March 14, 1861) Under slavery, we live surrounded by prostitutes, yet an abandoned woman is sent out of any decent house. Who thinks any worse of a Negro or mulatto woman for being a thing we can't name? God forgive us, but ours is a monstrous system, a wrong and an iniquity! Like the patriarchs of old, our men live all in one house with their wives and their concubines; and the mulattoes one sees in every [black] family partly resemble the white children. Any lady is ready to tell you who is the father of all the mulatto children in everybody's household but her own. Those, she seems to think, drop from the clouds. My disgust sometimes is boiling over. . . .

(August 22, 1861) I hate slavery. You say there are no more fallen women on a plantation than in London, in proportion to numbers, but what do you say to this? A magnate [person of power] who runs a hideous black harem with its consequences under the same roof with his lovely white wife and accomplished daughters?"

The abolitionists disagreed among themselves over what course of action to take against slavery and what to do for African Americans when they were finally freed. Some abolitionists advocated armed rebellion and war, while others pursued peaceful political paths. Henry Garnet, a former slave, openly preached violence and the killing of all slave masters. Frederick Douglass and Sojourner Truth, also former slaves, used lecture platforms and newspapers to bring about peaceful change. Abraham Lincoln hoped that stopping the expansion of slavery into the new states would cause slavery to gradually die out. He thought that transporting free blacks to Liberia, a newly formed country in West Africa, would defuse a lot of the social problems he foresaw in the nation. David Herbert Donald, a Lincoln biographer, writes, "Lincoln thought voluntary emigration of the blacks . . . would succeed both in 'freeing our land from the dangerous presence of slavery' and 'in restoring a captive people to their long-lost fatherland, with bright prospects for the future.'"[48]

The emigrationist movement proved to be an unrealistic solution. There were no money or ships to carry freed blacks back to Africa. Besides, many blacks rejected the idea; they had been born in the United States and felt little connection to Africa. Eventually fifteen thousand immigrated to Liberia, but few survived long; many became ill before they were able to create a rudimentary settlement. Sickness, a lack of supplies, and poor relations with the uncooperative natives all besieged the Liberian colonists.

The debate over slavery grew stronger and stronger in the years preceding the Civil War. Lincoln gave his most eloquent statement against slavery in his famous "House Divided" speech, in which he declared:

> I do not expect the Union to be dissolved—I do not expect the House to fall—but I do expect it to cease to be divided. It will become all one thing or all the other. Either the opponents of slavery will arrest the further spread of it, and place it where the public mind shall rest in the belief that it is in the course of ultimate extinction; or its advocates will push it forward, til it shall become alike lawful in all the States, old as well as new, North as well as South.[49]

Abolitionist John Brown is led to the gallows after his failed attempt to raid a federal arsenal, start a rebellion, and free the slaves.

Signs for runaway slaves were common in border states near the North such as Maryland. Slavery sharply divided the nation and was a contributing factor to the Civil War.

In October 1859 a Kansas abolitionist, John Brown, led a small band of twenty-one men on a raid of a federal arsenal at Harpers Ferry, Virginia. He intended to capture the arms stored there, hide in the mountains, and launch a rebellion that would liberate all slaves. The raid failed. Only five of his men escaped. Ten were killed and the rest, including Brown, were later hanged. John Brown became a martyr for the abolitionists, who had refused to join in his futile plan, but now marched in his name. The Civil War officially began when Confederate artillery fired on the federal Fort Sumter in the harbor of Charleston, South Carolina, on April 12, 1861. But to many observers, John Brown had fired the first shots in the war that would abolish slavery in America.

The Civil War

Whatever other differences existed between the northern states of the Union and the eleven southern states that broke away and formed their own Confederate States of America in 1860 and 1861, the issue of slavery dominated the agenda. The slave states wanted to preserve the right to choose if they wanted slavery. They knew the newly elected president, Abraham Lincoln, was opposed to slavery. Lincoln saw the secession of southern states as a rebellion and fought to keep the nation together as one society. He had no authority to interfere with slavery within any state, but he encouraged the states to work toward abolishing slavery gradually on their own. But as the war entered its second year with a mounting cost in lives and money, the abolitionists stepped up their pressure on Lincoln to end slavery by edict. After months of deliberation, the Emancipation Proclamation came into effect on January 1, 1863. The edict freed slaves in the Confederate states, but it had little effect until the Union army could conquer southern territory and liberate the slaves.

As they had in the Revolutionary War and the War of 1812 against England, free blacks joined the army as soon as they were allowed in. Altogether a half million of them fought or worked for the Union army, and thirty-eight thousand died in the war. Soon after the Confederate army

Slave Religion

In Roll Jordan Roll: The World the Slaves Made, *historian Eugene Genovese quotes from an article in the* Southern Cultivator, *an agricultural magazine that was circulated among planters and overseers during 1840–1860.*

"Another fact, equally notorious, is that on almost every large plantation of Negroes there is one among them who holds a kind of magical sway over the minds and opinions of the rest; to him they look as their oracle—and this same oracle, thought most generally a preacher, is, in ninety-nine cases out of a hundred, the most consummate villain and hypocrite on the premises. It is more likely that he has seen sundry [various] miraculous visions; . . . angels have talked with him, etc., etc. The influence of such a negro on the [slave] quarter is incalculable. He steals his master's pigs, and is still an object commanding the peculiar regard of Heaven, and why may not his disciples? It may be, and in most cases this influence is, such an obstacle in the way of the missionary, that he can accomplish little unless his preaching is in unison with the theology of this sage old Doctor of Divinity."

Slaves, some wearing captured Union uniforms, plant sweet potatoes on a South Carolina plantation during the Civil War.

surrendered in 1865, the reunited United States passed three constitutional amendments abolishing slavery and giving blacks equal rights as citizens. But the end of slavery in the United States was not the end of slavery in the world.

The last western power to maintain slavery was Brazil, where emancipation did not come until 1888. Yet slavery has persisted, legal or illegal, around the world. Bonded laborers, including small children, are often the technical equivalent of slaves, and they exist by the thousands. Human beings are still bought and sold. Poverty, economic inequality, and governments unresponsive to human rights violations continue to create fertile ground for slavery to exist.

7 The Persistence of Slavery

In 1978 Syed Riaz Hussain Shah, a horti-culturist formerly of Florida's Miami Dade Community College, pleaded guilty in federal court to holding a person in "involuntary servitude." He and his wife, anesthesiologist Isharad Majed Shah, purchased an African girl, Rose Iftony, from Sierra Leone for two hundred dollars, promising her mother that they would educate the girl. At the time they purchased Rose, the Shahs were registered aliens from Pakistan. The couple kept Rose as a house slave for at least two years. Rose had

only one dress to wear; she ate rice from a tin plate, and she drank from a broken glass. An FBI agent referred to her bondage as "the first classic case of slavery [in the United States] this century that the F.B.I. knows of."[50]

According to Great Britain's Anti-Slavery International, the world's oldest human rights organization, there are more than 200 million slaves in the world today. Despite the 1948 United Nations Universal Declaration of Human Rights, which decreed that "no one shall be held

This mother, son, and daughter work as slaves packing eucalyptus logs into kilns in Brazil. More than 200 million slaves are estimated in the world today.

Modern slaves include child laborers, like these carpet weavers, who are easily exploited and made to work under horrible conditions.

in slavery or servitude; slavery and the slave trade shall be prohibited in all their forms," slavery continues. So-called employment contracts and fake marriages are used to make what is really slavery appear legitimate.

The estimated number of slaves is even larger when the word *slave* is used to describe anyone who is unable to withdraw his or her labor voluntarily. This definition includes bonded laborers, who work for nothing to pay off moneylenders; serfs, who cannot leave the agricultural estates where they work; and exploited children, who are cut off from their families to work long hours for low wages or no wages at all.

Anti-Slavery International estimates that more than 5 million bonded laborers exist in India alone. Because children there can inherit the debts of their parents, it is possible to see three generations working side by side in the stone quarries outside Delhi. These bonded laborers often come from minority groups.

Eighty percent of India's bonded laborers are from the lowest caste, called the untouchables.

Child Slavery

Bonded children work in sweatshop conditions throughout Asia and Latin America. Child workers are cheap, exploitable, and expendable. Children who work in Pakistani carpet factories knot rugs in crowded, dark shops with little ventilation. They work for as many as sixteen hours a day, seven days a week, hand tying the thousands of knots that make up carpets. Often chained to their looms, the children sleep in the factories after the work is done. They suffer deep cuts on their hands from the knives used to cut the wool from the knot, and the dust and fluff from the wool bring on lung diseases. Some are paid a couple of cents a day; others receive nothing. The children who

Carpet Slaves

In an article called "Slavery: Worldwide Evil," taken from the monthly magazine World & I, *Charles Jacobs, research director of the American Anti-Slavery Group, writes about the life of one carpet slave in India.*

"Five year old Santosh was playing with friends in his village in Bahar, India when a group of men rode up in a jeep and offered to take the children to a movie. Instead, they were driven 400 miles to Allahabad—the heart of India's 'carpet belt'—and sold into slavery. Locked into a room and given no food until he agreed to weave on the looms, Santosh made oriental carpets for nine years, working from 4 am in the morning to 11 pm at night, every day, without breaks. He was never given a single rupee for his labor. When he cut his finger with a sharp tool, the loom master shaved match heads into the cut and set the sulfur on fire. He didn't want the child's blood staining the carpet. After he was rescued, the director of the International Labor Rights and Education Fund described Santosh as '. . . almost catatonic. He had practically no emotion left in him.'"

try to leave are tortured or even killed, and the rest live in constant fear of their masters.

Iqbal Malish was four years old when his mother sold him to such a factory for twelve dollars. At age ten he escaped and spent the next two years encouraging other children to do the same. Through his efforts he helped to free as many as three thousand other bonded child laborers. In 1994 Iqbal received the Reebok Human Rights Youth in Action Award, and traveled to Boston, Massachusetts, to accept it. Four months later Iqbal was shot to death in Pakistan while riding a bicycle. He was twelve years old. His assassins were never found.

The Indian Bonded Labor Liberation Front believes that between two hundred thousand and three hundred thousand children are involved in the handmade woolen carpet industry, which is one of the largest export industries in the country. Children become carpet slaves in several ways. Some inherit debt from their parents and become bonded slaves; others are kidnapped, simply stolen off the streets; while still others are given over to a labor contractor who promises that the child will be educated and cared for while learning a trade. To help stop the use of child slave labor in the making of carpets, a consortium of European and Asian rights groups began the Rugmark Campaign, which licenses carpet exporters and manufacturers who do not use child labor. Rugs made by these licensed groups are given a "Rugmark"—an official label that certifies the carpet was not made using child labor.

Asian children are also exploited and enslaved in the international sex trade, which flourishes in Southeast Asia. In some Thai villages girls are dragged out of school as early as the sixth grade and taken to the brothels of Bangkok. "At 10 you are a woman," according to a popular saying in Bangkok's red-light district. "At 20 you are an old woman. At 30 you are dead."[51] According to Christine Vertucci, information officer with End Child Prostitution in Asian Tourism (ECPAT), the international sex trade is centered in Thailand but has spread throughout Asia, where girls as young as eight years old are sold into prostitution. Hundreds of thousands of Asian boys and girls have been put to work in brothels. Like the carpet-factory children, many of these children are sold outright by their parents, who may have been lured by promises of decent employment for their children. Others are kidnapped or caught in debt bondage.

In Port-au-Prince, Haiti, as in many other underdeveloped nations, the poor exploit the children of those with even less income than themselves by adopting them and using them as unpaid domestic servants. In Haiti these children are called *restaveks*, or "stay-withs," and they often wear rags, eat scraps, and sleep on the

A child prostitute sits with her pimp in Thailand, the center of the international sex trade in Asia.

ground. Four-year-old Woodcaby Dieu-juste was adopted by a family in Port-au-Prince. His day now begins at 6 A.M., when he empties the chamber pot, builds a fire, fetches water from the well, and cooks breakfast. He goes to sleep at 9:30 P.M., sometimes with no dinner. He wears a pair of dirty pants and receives no pay. He does not go to school and will probably never again see his parents, who have moved on. Woodcaby misses his parents but is happy "because I want to be,"[52] he says.

Children also continue to be exploited and enslaved in Mauritania and the Sudan, where a history of Arab enslavement of Africans continues to this day.

Slavery in Sudan and Mauritania

The northern African country of Sudan has been torn apart by civil war, as Muslim authorities in the region bordering the Islamic nations of Libya and Egypt have attempted to impose *sharia*, or Islamic law, in the southern part of the country. Sudan is divided ethnically into the northern Muslims, who are of Arab extraction, and the southern Christians and animists (people who follow traditional African forms of nature worship), who are black. A civil war in which the non-Muslim groups are struggling for autonomy has left tens of thousands of orphaned southern Sudanese children who must find their own food and shelter. Thousands more have been abducted from their homes and sold as slaves. Human beings who have been treated in this fashion are said to be the victims of chattel slavery. Some are forced to serve as household servants, concubines, or field-workers. Some are branded like cattle. Others are confined in work camps and leased to private landowners. There are frequent reports that slaves are being exported to other North African

Boys and girls in Southeast Asia are kidnapped or sold by their parents and forced to work in brothels like these.

Villages Haunted by Slavery

In 1996, the Baltimore Sun newspaper sent two reporters to Sudan. There they found shocking evidence of slavery tearing apart Sudan's black population. The reporters told the story of Dur Dut Kuot, a sixty-year-old man who managed to escape from his captors when his village was raided for slaves.

"[Dur Dut Kuot] was tending his tobacco field by the river, outside the village of Makuei, when he heard an enemy raiding party was on the rampage. He dropped his watering can and ran off to hide. But an enemy horseman found him in the undergrowth. 'He pointed his rifle at me,' [Kuot] recalled. 'I was sure I was going to die.' Captured, he and the other prisoners were herded along during the day and tied up at night. For five days he carried two full sacks of looted clothes and a kidnapped child. 'A lot of children were with us. Two of them died on the way,' he said. . . . In a town called Shengat, the human booty was distributed. 'I realized I was becoming a slave. We were all there, and anyone who wanted you could call you. All the slaves were one group, women, children, men all together. Everyone could take whatever kind of person they wanted. Anyone who likes women could take women. Anyone who likes girls could take girls. Anyone who likes a small boy could take a small boy.'"

and Persian Gulf countries. Those who try to escape are beaten, mutilated, or murdered. While the government of Sudan denies the existence of slavery within its borders, the firsthand testimony of escaped slaves indicates that the officials are lying.

In the Islamic Republic of Mauritania, drought, poverty, and unemployment, combined with racial discrimination, have led tens of thousands of Africans into slavery. Many of these slaves are themselves the descendants of slaves. Even former slaves, those who supposedly have been freed, continue to be worked as slaves under the auspices of a "labor contract." Slaves in Mauritania are not allowed to marry, have a family, attend school, or practice their religions. Although the government has outlawed slavery several times, most recently in 1980, it has never passed any laws to punish slave owners. According to Rakiya Omaar, executive director of the human rights organization Africa Watch: "Although slaves are no longer sold on the open market . . . sales continue through discreet arrangements, such as 'exchanges' or they are given as lifelong 'presents.' Slaves remain the property of the master's family, without

These two Sudanese boys were kidnapped and enslaved by Muslims in northern Sudan. The northern Muslims put kidnapped black Sudanese to work as domestic slaves, concubines, or field-workers.

any legal rights."[53] Most slaves, descendants of the Africans conquered by Arabs during the twelfth century, have never heard anything about the 1980 law abolishing slavery. All of the slaves in Mauritania are Africans, enslaved by Arabs. They cultivate the land, collect water, and perform domestic chores. A *beydanne*—a white man or Arab—does not perform these tasks.

A teacher in the Tagant region, who was deported from Mauritania in 1989, describes how even ex-slaves, or *haratines*, continue to be worked as slaves:

No one can tell me that slavery is dead in Mauritania. I found an old and well-established social order in which everyone had their place, clearly marked. After five years of seeing for myself the life of slaves, it is clear to me that it is meaningless to draw a distinction between the "haratine of X" and the "slave of X." The difference exists only in the language, not in the reality. The center of the social order is the white master who has the right to do nothing while the blacks do all

the work. When the master goes to the fields, he usually sits in the shade of a tree and is served tea while the blacks do all the work. No white woman does any domestic work. All household tasks are done by slave women who have grown up in the household.[54]

Since a severe drought struck Mauritania in the early 1970s, large numbers of people have been forced off the land and into the cities, where they compete for employment and add to the market for slaves. Racial discrimination and lack of education, together with Mauritania's poor economy, have made it difficult for ex-slaves to establish an economic footing and find work for themselves. As a result, many fall back into slavery. Both a UN special investigation team and the antislavery society have recommended that the Mauritanian government give loans to help these former slaves purchase livestock or start businesses, and that it establish schools.

In 1974 former slaves, known as *haratines*, founded a group dedicated to consciousness-raising among slaves and to improving the lives of former slaves.

Called El Hor, the group took its name from the Arabic word for freedom. El Hor argued that emancipation was useless unless former slaves had the means to gain their economic independence, so the movement was committed to land reform and to the establishment of agricultural cooperatives for *haratines*. According to Africa Watch, the government of Mauritania was embarrassed by the negative publicity El Hor's activities attracted and attempted to suppress the group. Today El

International Kidnapping Rings

According to Bangladeshi professor Abdul Momen, quoted in the Anti-Slavery Report, *an international kidnapping ring is being run in Bangladesh by people who represent themselves as labor contractors.*

"'Jamila promised [said one mother] that my daughter would get a good-paying job. I believed her. I know families in this village who get money each month from their children working in the Middle East. I believed her.' And so, the mother explained, she sent her daughter off and never heard from her again. Now she lives in terror of rumors that Bangladeshi girls are made slaves, become the 'wives' of sheiks and are sold into brothels. The rumors are true.

In 1992, Abdul Momen, a native of Bangladesh, now a professor at Merrimac College, interviewed parents from villages in Bangladesh where over 1,000 young girls disappeared after going off with 'labor contractors.' Momen's investigation led him to conclude that a network of child slavers supplies girls and boys to Asian brothels and Middle East potentates [royalty]. The girls are used to stock the bordellos in Pakistan and India, or are sold into the Persian Gulf as sex slaves, maids, and 'wives.' Little boys are shipped off to the Gulf where they are trained to be jockeys in the national pastime of several Persian Gulf states—camel racing. . . . They grow up, live, and die as slaves.

Over 600,000 impoverished Bangladeshis work in the Gulf states and the money they send their families back home amounts to a billion dollars each year. This is a significant portion of Bangladesh's annual budget. According to Momen, efforts to stop the slave trade are thwarted by Bangladeshi officials who don't want to 'annoy the Gulf states' with complaints about the theft of their country's children. They fear the slaving states might retaliate by limiting the number of Bangladeshis who can work there."

Hor is not a strong political force; its members are afraid to meet openly or demonstrate for fear of violent reprisals.

The government of Mauritania has refused to release census figures for the past two decades, and blacks believe this is because the population data illustrates that *beydannes* are actually the minority in the country.

Public Response

There has been almost no support for the protest against slavery in the Sudan or Mauritania. Even the African-American organizations that so vocally campaigned against apartheid, or racial segregation, in South Africa have remained silent on the issue of slavery. When Mohamed Athie of the International Coalition Against Chattel Slavery asked to speak about the crisis of slavery in Africa at the Million Man March in Washington, D.C., in 1996, organizer Louis Farrakhan of the Nation of Islam refused the human rights worker's request. Moreover, the Congressional Black Caucus failed to back a resolution introduced by Massachusetts Democratic congressman Barney Frank that would require the U.S. government to act against slave-trading nations by employing economic sanctions, withholding foreign aid, or other measures.

The existence of slavery in northern Africa is rationalized by some in the name

These two boys were kidnapped and forced to work as slaves in a field for six years.

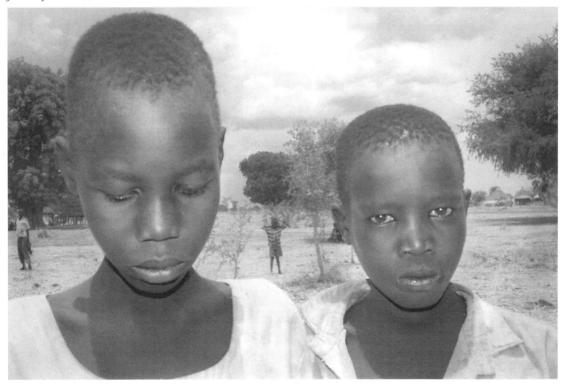

of culture. No one wants to point the finger at Islamic slaving nations and say that what they are doing is wrong. As a result of these cultural differences, some governments believe that human rights standards should vary from country to country. Increasingly, although not in every case, the world community has refused to accept blatant human rights violations, and intervention in situations where human rights are not respected is more likely now than it was in the past. For example, the atrocities of the Bosnian war compelled the United Nations to act against Serb aggression, and in response to Iraqi harassment of the Kurds, the United States created a safe-haven zone for the Kurdish minority in Iraq.

The practice of slavery has gradually become more isolated and less common than ever before; for the first time, slavery has been reduced to only a few areas of the world. Yet the persistence of slavery in the modern world calls into question the notion of human progress. Abolitionists around the world encourage consumers to boycott products made with forced labor and not to do business with or travel to countries where slavery exists. By pressuring the governments of countries where slave practices still exist, other countries can attempt to stop the spread of slavery and work toward its extinction. The long history of human slavery shows us that, at different times, virtually all cultures have been the slavers or the enslaved. To finish slavery's long and gradual extinction, many different cultures will have to agree on a definition of human rights and work to create a climate where freedom can survive.

Notes

Chapter 1: Slavery in Early Mediterranean Civilizations

1. Quoted in M. I. Finley, *Ancient Slavery and Modern Ideology*. New York: Viking, 1980, p. 12.

2. Hans Baumann, *In the Land of Ur: The Discovery of Ancient Mesopotamia*. Trans. Stella Humphries. New York: Pantheon Books, 1969, pp. 92–93.

3. Herodotus, *The Histories*. Trans. Aubrey de Sélincourt. Baltimore: Penguin Classics, 1960, p. 151.

4. Quoted in Dimitris Kyratatas, "The Athenian Democracy and Its Slaves," *History Today*, February 1994, p. 47.

5. Quoted in James Walvin, *Slavery and the Slave Trade*. Jackson: University Press of Mississippi, 1983, p. 5.

6. Walvin, *Slavery and the Slave Trade*, pp. 8–9.

7. Israel E. Levine, *The Many Faces of Slavery*. New York: J. Messner, 1975, p. 74.

8. Quoted in Keith Hopkins, *Conquerors and Slaves*. New York: Cambridge University Press, 1977, p. 121.

9. William D. Phillips Jr., *Slavery from Roman Times to the Early Transatlantic Trade*. Minneapolis: University of Minnesota Press, 1985, pp. 38–39.

Chapter 2: Slavery During the Middle Ages

10. Quoted in Phillips, *Slavery*, p. 98.

11. Anthony G. Hopkins, *An Economic History of West Africa*. New York: Macmillan, 1973, p. 86.

12. Arthur J. Arberry, trans., *The Koran Interpreted*. New York: Macmillan, 1964, *sura* 24, sec. 30, 2:5.

13. Quoted in Henry Hart, *Marco Polo: Venetian Adventurer*. Palo Alto, CA: Stanford University Press, 1942, p. 19.

14. Michel Balard, *Genes et l'Outre-Mer I: Les Actes de Caffa du Notaire Lamberto di Sambuceto, 1289–1290*. Paris: Mouton, 1973, pp. 85, 86, 198, 276, 334. Translations by the author.

15. Balard, *Genes et l'Outre-Mer*, p. 374.

16. Phillips, *Slavery*, pp. 98–99.

17. Balard, *Genes et l'Outre-Mer*, p. 273.

Chapter 3: Slavery in Africa

18. Quoted in Phillips, *Slavery*, p. 147.

19. Quoted in Leda Farant, *Tippu Tip and the East African Slave Trade*. New York: St. Martins Press, 1975, p. 19.

20. Quoted in Ivor Wilks, *Forests of Gold: Essays on the Akan and the Kingdom of Asante*. Athens: Ohio University Press, 1993, p. 226.

21. Phillips, *Slavery*, p. 83.

22. Phillips, *Slavery*, p. 83.

23. Quoted in Farant, *Tippu Tip*, pp. 8–9.

24. Philip D. Curtin, *Cross-Cultural Trade in World History*. Cambridge, England: Cambridge University Press, 1984, p. 37.

25. Quoted in Wilks, *Forests of Gold*, pp. 13–14.

Chapter 4: Indian Slavery in the Americas

26. Quoted in Brian M. Fagan, *The Aztecs*. New York: W. H. Freeman, 1984, pp. 177–78.

27. Lois Warburton, *Aztec Civilization*. San Diego: Lucent Books, 1995, p. 70.

28. Charles Gallenkamp, *Maya: The Riddle and Rediscovery of a Lost Civilization*. New York: Viking, 1985, p. 109.

29. Quoted in Robert H. Ruby and John A. Brown, *The Chinook Indians*. Norman: University of Oklahoma Press, 1988, p. 10.

30. Ruby and Brown, *The Chinook Indians*, p. 10.

31. Quoted in Ruby and Brown, *The Chinook Indians*, p. 116.

32. Quoted in David Brion Davis, *Slavery and Human Progress*. New York: Oxford University Press, 1984, p. 74.

Chapter 5: Europeans Enslave Indians and Africans in the Caribbean and South America

33. Quoted in Tzvetan Todorov, *The Conquest of America*. Trans. Richard Howard. New York: HarperCollins, 1982, p. 141.

34. Quoted in Todorov, *The Conquest of America*, p. 142.

35. Quoted in Walvin, *Slavery and the Slave Trade*, p. 44.

36. Quoted in Walvin, *Slavery and the Slave Trade*, p. 54.

37. Quoted in Walvin, *Slavery and the Slave Trade*, pp. 76–77.

38. C. L. R. James, *The Black Jacobins: Toussaint L'Ouverture and the San Domingo Revolution*. New York: Vintage Press, 1989, pp. 12–13.

39. Quoted in George Francis Dow, *Slave Ships and Slaving*. Port Washington, NY: Kennikat Press, 1927, p. 247.

40. Esteban Montejo, *The Autobiography of a Runaway Slave*. Ed. Miguel Barnet, trans. Jocasta Innes. New York: Pantheon, 1968.

Chapter 6: Slavery in the American Colonies and the United States

41. Quoted in William B. Weeden, *Economic and Social History of New England, 1620–1789*, vol. 1. Boston: Houghton Mifflin, 1891, p. 149.

42. Quoted in Dow, *Slave Ships and Slaving*, p. 261.

43. Letter to John Francis Mercer, September 9, 1786, Pierpont Morgan Library Collection, New York.

44. Thomas Jefferson, *Notes*. Ed. William Peden. Chapel Hill: University of North Carolina Press, 1955, p. 1162.

45. Quoted in Nancy Cott, *Root of Bitterness*. Boston: Northeastern University Press, 1986, p. 189.

46. Letter to the Marquis de Lafayette, November 25, 1820, Pierpont Morgan Library Collection, New York.

47. Letter to Lydia Howard Sigourney, July 18, 1824, Pierpont Morgan Library Collection, New York.

48. David Herbert Donald, *Lincoln*. New York: Simon & Schuster, 1995, p. 162.

49. Quoted in Mary Beth Norton et al., *A People and a Nation*, vol. 1. Boston: Houghton Mifflin, 1990, p. 390.

Chapter 7: The Persistence of Slavery

50. Alton Hornsby Jr., *Milestones in Twentieth Century Black American History*. Detroit: Visible Ink Press, 1993, p. 291.

51. Bob Hebert, "Kids for Sale," *New York Times*, January 28, 1996, p. A15.

52. "Slavery," *Newsweek*, May 4, 1992, p. 39.

53. Rakiya Omaar, "The Forgotten Slaves," *Christian Science Monitor*, August 14, 1990.

54. "Mauritania: Slavery, Alive and Well, 10 Years After It Was Abolished," *News from Africa Watch*, June 29, 1990, p. 10.

For Further Reading

Hans Baumann, *In the Land of Ur: The Discovery of Ancient Mesopotamia.* Trans. Stella Humphries. New York: Pantheon Books, 1969. The story of the region where Western civilization began.

Colin G. Calloway, *North Country Captives.* Hanover, NH: University Press of New England, 1992. Accounts of European settlers who were captured by Native Americans and ransomed back to their countrymen.

Philip D. Curtin, *Cross-Cultural Trade in World History.* Cambridge, England: Cambridge University Press, 1984. A history of commercial encounters between civilizations, from the silk and spice trade between Rome and China to the transatlantic trade.

Leda Farant, *Tippu Tip and the East African Slave Trade.* New York: St. Martin's Press, 1975. A biography of one of the most infamous characters in the East African–Arab slave network and a history of the slave trade in the region during the nineteenth century.

Charles Gallenkamp, *Maya: The Riddle and Rediscovery of a Lost Civilization.* New York: Viking, 1985. Written by a museum curator, *Maya* details the origins, rise, and collapse of the Mayan Empire and analyzes material culture found during archaeological excavations.

Eugene D. Genovese, *Roll Jordan Roll: The World the Slaves Made.* New York: Vintage Press, 1976. A social history of the plantation life of slaves, detailing the lives of slave children and adults, as well as slave religion, work ethics, traditions, resistance, and revolt.

Thomas Hoobler and Dorothy Hoobler, *Toussaint L'Ouverture.* New York: Chelsea House, 1990. A biography of the leader of the Haitian slave revolt and a history of this event.

June Namias, *White Captives.* Chapel Hill: University of North Carolina Press, 1993. A study of white males and females who were taken captive by various Indian groups in America and of how historical accounts of their captivity reflect ideas about race, gender, and culture.

Lois Warburton, *Aztec Civilization.* San Diego: Lucent Books, 1995. Describes everyday life and culture among the Aztecs, explains how the Aztecs utilized slave labor, and discusses the nature of slavery in the Aztec Empire.

Works Consulted

Arthur J. Arberry, trans., *The Koran Interpreted*. New York: Macmillan, 1964. English translation of the Koran, with notes to help readers.

Michel Balard, *Genes et l'Outre-Mer I: Les Actes de Caffa du Notaire Lamberto di Sambuceto, 1289–1290*. Paris: Mouton, 1973. Records of sale from the notebooks of the notary of Kaffa, where the largest medieval slave market took place. Entries describe slaves, their buyers and sellers, and sale prices. In French.

Russel Bourne, *The Red King's Rebellion*. New York: Atheneum, 1990. Discusses racial politics in seventeenth-century New England and explains how some settlers sold Native Americans into slavery.

Christopher Brooke, *Europe in the Central Middle Ages, 962–1154*. New York: Longman, 1964. Refers to the European slave trade and the heavy raiding of the Slavic countries.

Michael D. Coe, *The Maya*. London: Thames and Hudson, 1987. History of the Mayan people, their practices, and the end of their empire.

Simon Collier, *From Cortéz to Castro: An Introduction to the History of Latin America, 1492–1973*. New York: Macmillan, 1974. Describes European attempts to enslave Indians, and later Africans, in Latin America and the treatment of plantation slaves.

M. A. Cook, ed., *Studies in the Economic History of the Middle East*. Oxford: Oxford University Press, 1970. Includes statistics on the slave trade and the numbers of slaves traded annually at the major markets, based on travel accounts and records of sale.

Nancy Cott, *Root of Bitterness*. Boston: Northeastern University Press, 1986. Contains documents on the social history of American women, including oral histories of former slaves.

David Brion Davis, *Slavery and Human Progress*. New York: Oxford University Press, 1984. A survey of slavery and emancipation throughout world history.

David Herbert Donald, *Lincoln*. New York: Simon & Schuster, 1995. A biography of the president including his writings.

George Francis Dow, *Slave Ships and Slaving*. Port Washington, NY: Kennikat Press, 1927. History of the slaving ships of New England, their owners and financiers, voyages, and home ports.

Diego Duran, *Book of the Gods and Rites and the Ancient Calendar*. Norman: University of Oklahoma Press, 1971. Discusses Aztec cosmology, astronomy, and astrology.

Robert B. Edgerton, *Sick Societies: Challenging the Myth of Primitive Harmony*. New York: Free Press, 1992. Investigates cultural practices that harm certain populations and discusses how these customs affect the society.

Brian M. Fagan, *The Aztecs*. New York: W. H. Freeman, 1984. An in-depth look at Aztec civilization, from customs to Aztec cosmology and astrology.

M. I. Finley, *Ancient Slavery and Modern Ideology*. New York: Viking, 1980. A discussion of the philosophies and causes of slavery from its beginnings.

J. H. Galloway, "The Mediterranean Sugar Industry," *Geographical Review*, 1977, pp. 177–94.

Henry Hart, *Marco Polo: Venetian Adventurer.* Palo Alto, CA: Stanford University Press, 1942. Biography of Marco Polo. Also a history of commercial activity in and around medieval Venice, including descriptions of the slave trade.

Bob Hebert, "Kids for Sale," *New York Times,* January 28, 1996, p. A15.

Richard Hellie, *Slavery in Russia.* Chicago: University of Chicago Press, 1982. History of slave routes and slave trading in southern Russia during the fifteenth century.

Herodotus, *The Histories.* Trans. Aubrey de Sélincourt. Baltimore: Penguin Classics, 1960. Greek historian-traveler's view of Greek history and Greece's conflicts with Persia. Also provides an astonishing array of facts, legends, and digressions about the geography, customs, and culture of the rest of the known world.

Anthony G. Hopkins, *An Economic History of West Africa.* New York: Macmillan, 1973. Discusses commerce and trading networks in West African history, including the role of the horse in trade.

Keith Hopkins, *Conquerors and Slaves.* New York: Cambridge University Press, 1977. Discusses Roman history, social structure, and the role of slaves.

Alton Hornsby Jr., *Milestones in Twentieth Century Black American History.* Detroit: Visible Ink Press, 1993. A chronology of important events in African-American history since 1900.

"International Kidnapping Rings Make Slaves of Asia's Children," *Anti-Slavery Report,* November 1994, p. 2.

Charles Jacobs, "Slavery: Worldwide Evil," *World & I,* April 1996, pp. 110–12.

C. L. R. James, *The Black Jacobins: Toussaint L'Ouverture and the San Domingo Revolution.* New York: Vintage Press, 1963. History of the slave revolt and political transformation of Haiti under Toussaint-Louverture.

Thomas Jefferson, *Notes.* Ed. William Peden. Chapel Hill: University of North Carolina Press, 1955.

John K. Jewitt, *The Northwest Coast Adventure of Captain John K. Jewitt.* Ed. Alice W. Shurecliff and Sarah Shurecliff Ingelfinger. Boston: Back Bay Books, 1993. An account of Jewitt's captivity among the Nootka Indians of the Pacific Northwest.

Dimitris Kyratatas, "The Athenian Democracy and Its Slaves," *History Today,* February 1994.

Ronald Latham, ed., *The Travels of Marco Polo.* London: Penguin Books, 1958. Travelogue of a medieval explorer and trader. Contains references to commodities traded along the Silk Route, including slaves.

Israel E. Levine, *The Many Faces of Slavery.* New York: J. Messner, 1975. Overview of slavery through history.

Bernard Lewis, *Race and Slavery in the Middle East.* New York: Oxford University Press, 1990. Historical inquiry into the nature of slavery in the world of Islam that explores representations of slaves in literature and art.

Gilbert A. Lewthwaite and Gregory Kane, "Horror in Villages Haunted by Slavery," *Baltimore Sun,* June 17, 1996, p. A-6.

"Mauritania: Slavery, Alive and Well 10 Years After It Was Abolished," *News from Africa Watch,* June 29, 1990, p. 10.

Milton Meltzer, *Slavery: A World History.* New York: Da Capo Press, 1993. The story of slavery from the rise of Western civilization to the late twentieth century.

Dorothy Mills, *The Book of the Ancient Romans.* New York: G. P. Putnam's Sons, 1937. An introduction to the history and civilization of Rome from the founding of the city to its decline.

Esteban Montejo, *The Autobiography of a Runaway Slave.* Ed. Miguel Barnet, trans. Jocasta Innes. New York: Pantheon, 1968. True story of an escaped slave.

Mary Beth Norton et al., *A People and a Nation,* vol. 1. Boston: Houghton Mifflin, 1990. A textbook of American history to 1877.

Rakiya Omaar, "The Forgotten Slaves," *Christian Science Monitor,* August 14, 1990.

William D. Phillips Jr., *Slavery from Roman Times to the Early Transatlantic Trade.* Minneapolis: University of Minnesota Press, 1985. Sweeping history of enslavement from the Roman Empire onwards, including slavery in the Islamic world and in the Middle Ages, up to the beginnings of the Atlantic slave trade.

Albert Raboteau, *Slave Religion.* New York: Oxford University Press, 1978. Documents the origins of slave religion and describes the development of African Christianity.

Robert H. Ruby and John A. Brown, *The Chinook Indians.* Norman: University of Oklahoma Press, 1988. Discusses the Chinookan-speaking Indian groups and their role as traders.

"Slavery," *Newsweek,* May 4, 1992, p. 39.

"Slavery, by Any Other Name," *The Economist,* January 6, 1990, p. 42.

Barbara Solow, "Capitalism and Slavery," *Journal of Interdisciplinary History,* vol. 17, 1987, pp. 711–37.

Tzvetan Todorov, *The Conquest of America.* Trans. Richard Howard. New York: HarperCollins, 1982. Explores the significance of the conquest of Mesoamerica by the Spaniards and the cultural differences between the Indians and the Spanish, including language and communication, concepts of time, and religion.

A. L. Udovitch, ed., *The Islamic Middle East, 700–1900: Studies in Economic and Social History.* Princeton, NJ: Darwin Press, 1981. Discusses the military slaves of the Mamluk sultanate and the markets at Kaffa.

A. Van Dantzig and A. Jones, *Pieter de Marees: A Description and Historical Account of the Gold Kingdom of Guinea, 1602.* Oxford: Oxford University Press, 1987. A description and history of West Africa in the 1600s.

James Walvin, *Slavery and the Slave Trade.* Jackson: University Press of Mississippi, 1983. Slavery from ancient times to the transatlantic trade.

William B. Weeden, *An Economic and Social History of New England, 1620–1789,* vol. 1. Boston: Houghton Mifflin, 1891. Nineteenth-century history of New England. Includes discussion of the triangle trade in rum, slaves, and molasses.

Ivor Wilks, *Forests of Gold: Essays on the Akan and the Kingdom of Asante.* Athens: Ohio University Press, 1993. History of West African political domains and of economic development; special emphasis on the gold mines of the Ashanti and the slave and gold trading network with Arabs and Europeans that supplied a labor force for the mines.

Bart Winer, *Life in the Ancient World.* New York: Random House, 1961. A description of the daily life of the people in ancient Mediterranean civilizations.

David Wiggins, "The Play of Slave Children in the Plantation Communities of the Old South," *Journal of Sport History,* vol. 7, no. 2, Summer 1980, p. 22–31.

Index

Picture Credits

Cover photo: Library of Congress

AP Photo/Baltimore Sun, Gilbert A. Lewthwaite, 96

AP/Wide World Photos, 88, 94

Archive Photos, 11, 27, 36, 37, 69, 70, 72, 74, 77, 83 (both), 85 (bottom)

Archive Photos/American Stock, 87

The Bettmann Archive, 31 (both), 33, 44, 62

Corbis-Bettmann, 16, 21, 22, 65, 68, 73, 85 (top)

© Donna DeCesare/Impact Visuals, 89

Library of Congress, 32, 56, 57, 58, 61, 64, 75, 79

© Heldur Netocny/Impact Visuals, 91, 92

North Wind Picture Archives, 15, 17, 19, 23, 26, 47, 49, 50, 80

Stock Montage, Inc., 20, 38, 40, 42, 45, 54, 63

UPI/Bettmann, 13

About the Authors

Norman L. Macht is the author of more than twenty books for young adults, including biographies of Supreme Court justices Clarence Thomas and Sandra Day O'Connor. He is the president of Choptank Syndicate, Inc., and lives in Baltimore, Maryland.

Mary Hull received her B.A. from Brown University in 1995. She is the author of several books for young adults, including *Rosa Parks: Civil Rights Leader* and *The Travels of Marco Polo*. Ms. Hull lives in Boston, Massachusetts, where she writes for businesses and educational publishers.